Dedication

I dedicate this book to these future stars — Motsamai, Tumelo, Molefe, Thato, Makgotso.

About the Series

The African Humanities Series is a partnership between the African Humanities Program (AHP) of the American Council of Learned Societies and academic publishers NISC (Pty) Ltd. The Series covers topics in African histories, languages, literatures, philosophies, politics and cultures. Submissions are solicited from Fellows of the AHP, which is administered by the American Council of Learned Societies and financially supported by the Carnegie Corporation of New York.

The purpose of the AHP is to encourage and enable the production of new knowledge by Africans in the five countries designated by the Carnegie Corporation: Ghana, Nigeria, South Africa, Tanzania, and Uganda. AHP fellowships support one year's work free from teaching and other responsibilities to allow the Fellow to complete the project proposed. Eligibility for the fellowship in the five countries is by domicile, not nationality.

Book proposals are submitted to the AHP editorial board which manages the peer review process and selects manuscripts for publication by NISC. In some cases, the AHP board will commission a manuscript mentor to undertake substantive editing and to work with the author on refining the final manuscript.

The African Humanities Series aims to publish works of the highest quality that will foreground the best research being done by emerging scholars in the five Carnegie designated countries. The rigorous selection process before the fellowship award, as well as AHP editorial vetting of manuscripts, assures attention to quality. Books in the series are intended to speak to scholars in Africa as well as in other areas of the world.

The AHP is also committed to providing a copy of each publication in the series to university libraries in Africa.

AHP Editorial Board Members as at January 2020

AHP Series Editors:
Professor Adigun Agbaje, University of Ibadan, Nigeria
Professor Emeritus Fred Hendricks, Rhodes University, South Africa

Consultant:
Professor Emeritus Sandra Barnes, University of Pennsylvania, USA (Anthropology)

Board Members:
1. Professor Akosua Adomako Ampofo, Institute of African Studies, Ghana (Gender Studies & Advocacy) (Vice President, African Studies Association of Africa)
2. Professor Kofi Anyidoho, University of Ghana, Ghana (African Studies & Literature) (Director, Codesria African Humanities Institute Program)
3. Professor Ibrahim Bello-Kano, Bayero University, Nigeria (Dept of English and French Studies)
4. Professor Sati Fwatshak, University of Jos, Nigeria (Dept of History & International Studies)
5. Professor Patricia Hayes, University of the Western Cape, South Africa (African History, Gender Studies and Visuality) (SARChI Chair in Visual History and Theory)
6. Associate Professor Wilfred Lajul, College of Humanities & Social Sciences, Makerere University, Uganda (Dept of Philosophy)
7. Professor Yusufu Lawi, University of Dar-es-Salaam, Tanzania (Dept of History)
8. Professor Bertram Mapunda, University of Dar es Salaam, Tanzania (Dept of Archaeology & Heritage Studies)
9. Professor Innocent Pikirayi, University of Pretoria, South Africa (Chair & Head, Dept of Anthropology & Archaeology)
10. Professor Josephat Rugemalira, University of Dar-es-Salaam, Tanzania (Dept of Foreign Languages & Linguistics)
11. Professor Idayat Bola Udegbe, University of Ibadan, Nigeria (Dept of Psychology)

Published in this series

Dominica Dipio, *Gender terrains in African cinema*, 2014

Ayo Adeduntan, *What the forest told me: Yoruba hunter, culture and narrative performance*, 2014

Sule E. Egya, *Nation, power and dissidence in third-generation Nigerian poetry in English*, 2014

Irikidzayi Manase, *White narratives: The depiction of post-2000 land invasions in Zimbabwe*, 2016

Pascah Mungwini, *Indigenous Shona philosophy: Reconstructive insights*, 2017

Sylvia Bruinders, *Parading respectability: The cultural and moral aesthetics of the Christmas Bands Movement in the Western Cape, South Africa*, 2017

Michael Andindilile, *The Anglophone literary-linguistic continuum: English and indigenous languages in African literary discourse*, 2018

Jeremiah Arowosegbe, *Claude E Ake: the making of an organic intellectual*, 2018

Romanus Aboh, *Language and the construction of multiple identities in the Nigerian novel*, 2018

Bernard Matolino, *Consensus as democracy in Africa*, 2018

Babajide Ololajulo, *Unshared Identity: Posthumous paternity in a contemporary Yoruba community*, 2018

De-Valera NYM Botchway, *Boxing is no cakewalk! Azumah 'Ring Professor' Nelson in the social history of Ghanaian boxing*, 2019

Dina Ligaga, *Women, visibility and morality in Kenyan popular media*, 2020.

Okaka Opio Dokotum, *Hollywood and Africa: Recycling the 'Dark Continent' myth, 1908–2020*, 2020

AFRICAN PERSONHOOD AND APPLIED ETHICS

MOTSAMAI MOLEFE

Published in South Africa on behalf of the African Humanities Program
by NISC (Pty) Ltd, PO Box 377, Makhanda, 6140, South Africa
www.nisc.co.za

First edition, first impression 2020
Publication © African Humanities Program 2020
Text © Motsamai Molefe 2020

All rights reserved. No part of this publication may be reproduced or transmitted in any form or by any means, electronic or mechanical, including photocopying, recording, or any information storage or retrieval system, without prior permission in writing from the publisher.

ISBN: 978-1-920033-69-9 (print)
ISBN: 978-1-920033-70-5 (PDF)
ISBN: 978-1-920033-71-2 (ePub)

Project manager: Peter Lague
Indexer: Sanet le Roux
Cover design: Advanced Design Group
Cover photographs: © Andrey Tsvetkov/Dreamstime.com (front),
   © imageBROKER/Alamy Stock Photo (back)

Printed in South Africa by Digital Action

The author and the publisher have made every effort to obtain permission for and acknowledge the use of copyright material. Should an inadvertent infringement of copyright have occurred, please contact the publisher and we will rectify omissions or errors in any subsequent reprint or edition.

Contents

Acknowledgements	viii
Preface	ix
INTRODUCTION	1
CHAPTER 1 Personhood as a moral theory	17
CHAPTER 2 Personhood and dignity in African moral-political thought	35
CHAPTER 3 Personhood and the equality of women in African philosophy	54
CHAPTER 4 The place of animals in African moral philosophy	75
CHAPTER 5 Personhood and development in African philosophy	92
CONCLUSION	114
BIBLIOGRAPHY	117
INDEX	133

Acknowledgements

The success of this work was made possible because of the assistance and support of a large number of people and organisations to whom I am eternally grateful. Space does not permit me to express my gratitude to all of them, but I am cognisant of and acknowledge each one.

The manuscript for this publication was prepared with the support of the African Humanities Fellowship Program established by the American Council of Learned Societies (ACLS) with a generous grant from the Carnegie Corporation of New York. My sincere thanks go to the African Humanities Program (AHP) Series Editors, Prof. Emeritus Fred Hendricks, Rhodes University, South Africa and Prof. Adigun Agbaje, University of Ibadan, Nigeria for their support and to Barbara van der Merwe of the AHP Secretariat for her professionalism, patience, and encouraging motivation.

Thanks are also due to the two anonymous reviewers of the manuscript. Their comments, criticisms and insights were instructive and helpful.

My gratitude also goes to the Govan Mbeki Centre and Development Centre at the University of Fort Hare which provided generous financial support that contributed to making publication of this book possible. Prof. Pumla Gqola deserves a special mention for her leadership and for supporting my research in African philosophy.

My sincere thanks to Thaddeus Metz, Bernard Matolino, and Shepherd Mpofu, for all the support, mentoring and conversations about my career and our work as academics. I will always appreciate their influence and support. My gratitude would be incomplete without my heartfelt thanks to my partner and friend Asithandile Zibaya for all the support and love in my journey as a scholar and writer. Thank you for believing in me and being my number one supporter.

I acknowledge and appreciate John Irvine for editing the manuscript. I am also grateful for all the administrative, financial and collegial support I received from my colleagues — Chris Allsobrook and Sakhathina Mnonopi, at the Centre of Leadership Ethics in Africa (CLEA) at Fort Hare. It is truly a blessing to work with you colleagues. I am grateful to the Department of Philosophy at Fort Hare for organising a writing retreat where I worked on the revisions of the book.

I thank you all!

Preface

I was motivated to write this book by the swelling criticisms against the idea of personhood in the literature. Scholars of African moral thought, like Anthony Oyowe, Mpho Tshivhase, and Kai Horsthemke, among others, have raised what they regard as devastating objections against the moral idea of personhood. The thrust of these objections is that the idea of personhood is implausible, and we should explore other indigenous axiological resources to articulate a sound moral-political system. Three of these criticisms of personhood stood out for me.

The first criticism is that it fails to embody a just social order, where both men and women are equal and are owed equal moral duties. The suggestion inherent in this criticism is that the idea of personhood is intrinsically patriarchal and imagines and reproduces gender-based social inequalities that advantage and prioritise men at the expense of women. The second criticism focuses on the question of animals, anthropocentrism and speciesism. The point of this criticism is that the idea of personhood cannot embody a sound animal ethics since it is essentially speceistic. The third criticism suggests that the idea of personhood fails to embody the feature of social egalitarianism since it is a performance-based ethical system. What all these criticisms have in common is that they suggest that the idea of personhood fails to offer a plausible account of a just social order.

I believe that these criticisms underestimate the theoretical richness of the idea of personhood. The purpose of this book is to expose the robustness of the moral view inherent in the discourse of personhood. To do this, the book begins by philosophically explicating the under-explored dual features of personhood, namely moral perfectionism and dignity, which unfolds the major insight of the book. The literature has been fixated on the moral perfectionist facet of personhood, tending to overlook its dignity facet. I address this imbalance by articulating a plausible theory of dignity inherent in the idea of personhood. In so doing, I show that the criticisms against the idea of personhood are misguided and misfire because they overlook the dignity facet of personhood, which I believe is sufficient cause to challenge the objections raised by scholars of African moral thought. To reveal the robustness of the idea of personhood and to offer reasons that explain why we should take it seriously, I explore three disparate applied ethics themes — women, animals and development.

In my view, two outcomes would vindicate the existence of this book. The first is if it manages to articulate a robust ethics of personhood that is characterised by the dual features of moral perfectionism and dignity, and satisfactorily motivates why we need to take these two facets seriously as a moral view. And, secondly, if it demonstrates the claim that the idea of personhood embodies a certain conception of dignity, which is best accounted for in terms of the capacity for sympathy.

The one problem that this book creates but does not solve revolves around the possible tension between the moral perfectionism of personhood and the idea of dignity it embodies. In the book, I simply think of these two facets as part of the ethics of personhood, which has resources to offer a robust moral view, and I hope I have successfully employed these two features of the ethics of personhood to reflect on disparate applied ethics themes. I intend, in my future work, to reflect on this possible tension and resolve it. At present, it suffices to appreciate that personhood has a sufficiently robust conception of dignity that can facilitate meaningful engagement with social, moral and political themes in African philosophy.

Introduction

This book is a contribution to African philosophy — specifically, in the field of African ethics and applied ethics. Its motivation and content emerge in the light of three considerations. The first consideration revolves around themes from a special issue published in the journal *Theoria: A Journal of Social and Political Theory* titled *African philosophy and Rights*, which I co-edited with my colleague Christopher Allsobrook (see Molefe and Allsobrook, 2018). The idea of personhood featured significantly in the special issue. It was interesting to notice that one author after another, in the special issue, pointed to the pivotal role played by the idea of personhood in the discourse of rights in African philosophy (see Chemhuru 2018a; Chimakonam and Nweke 2018; Masaka 2018; Matolino 2018a). From this observation, I was struck by the insight that the idea of personhood could possibly be useful in dealing with a broad range of themes in applied ethics, beyond the fixation on idea of rights. Hence, this book focuses on applied ethics. In doing so, I select specific themes in applied ethics — largely those that are under-explored in the light of personhood in the tradition of African philosophy.[1]

The second consideration involves the specific direction of this book, which was influenced by the comments I received from the reviewers of the book's precursor — a proposal focused on human rights. One complaint that stood out was that although my interest in pursuing the discourse on rights was interesting, it did not embody the novelty usually associated with monographs. In response to this challenging criticism, this book endeavours to break new ground by focusing on a personhood-based conception of dignity.

It begins by offering a philosophical exposition of the axiological resources inherent in the discourse on personhood. It will do so specifically by philosophically explicating the dual features of the ethics of personhood, namely: moral perfection [self-realisation] and moral status/dignity. The tendency in the literature is to focus on the facet of moral perfection. I believe a robust conception of the ethics of personhood must appreciate and not ignore the role of moral status/dignity inherent in the idea of personhood. The next move involves the extension of the scope of discussion in the literature on personhood to themes in applied ethics, which are generally under-explored. Tersely, the aim is to articulate an under-explored conception of dignity inherent in the moral idea of personhood, and further use it to offer a unified account of applied ethics by applying it to questions relating to women, animals and development in African philosophy.

Introduction

The third consideration shaping this book's motivation and content is the lack of a book devoted to applied ethics in African philosophy, at least in the fashion imagined here of providing a unified account of disparate themes in applied ethics. One tends to find themes and concepts of moral and applied ethics like rights, animals, women, development, environmental ethics, business ethics, democracy, capital punishment, bioethics and so on, scattered in anthologies and journals, published both in Africa and globally, and approached in different ways (see Gyekye and Wiredu 1992; Murove 2009; Chimakonam and Nweke 2018). This book is an attempt to respond to this lacuna by philosophically and systematically pursuing a range of applied ethics themes — i.e. women, animals and development — in the African-philosophic tradition through the idea of personhood and the view of dignity it embodies.

Through its appeal to personhood and its view of dignity, I believe this book makes a positive contribution to discourses on the idea of personhood, African ethics and applied ethics, and that it will be useful largely to postgraduate students and academics. In what remains of this chapter, I provide the reader with a bird's eye perspective of the book's content. I begin by discussing the idea(s) of personhood central to this project. I then proceed to explain how I understand the idea of applied ethics, before considering the status of the literature concerning the themes mentioned above. I also explain how and why I have selected these themes. Finally, I outline the content of the remaining chapters. Let us begin.

The idea(s) of personhood in African philosophy

The idea of personhood in African philosophy is characterised by ambiguity, and often confusion. Scholars of African thought tend to distinguish between ontological and normative concepts of personhood (Wiredu 1996a, 2008, 2009; Gyekye 1992; Ikuenobe 2006, 2015, 2016; Oyowe 2013, 2014a, 2018; Matolino 2014; Molefe 2019a, 2019b). The ontological idea of personhood deals with the fact of being human. In analysing it, we philosophically explicate the descriptive features that constitute human nature (see Gyekye 1995; Kaphagawani 2004; Wiredu 2009; Ikuenobe 2015). It is crucial to understand that this ontological concept of personhood — in some fundamental sense — is prior and informs all other notions of personhood to be considered in what follows. I will say something about the normative idea of personhood below.

One of the leading scholars of African philosophy, Thaddeus Metz (2013a, 13), in his analysis of the debate between Ifeanyi Menkiti and Kwame Gyekye, identifies three distinct concepts of personhood, namely: the ideas of (1) personal identity; (2) moral status; and (3) moral virtue. The reader should notice that, in the light of this comment drawn from Metz, we have now specified four concepts of personhood, namely: personhood as a reference to (1) being human; (2) personal identity;

(3) moral status; and (4) moral virtue. In my own analysis of the debate between Menkiti and Gyekye, I come to the same conclusion as Metz — that there is a lack of precision regarding which notion of personhood is pivotal in proffering a plausible interpretation of Afro-communitarian moral and political thought (Molefe 2016, 2018, 2019a, Chapter 1). Below, I focus on the notions of personhood that I believe are crucial for Afro-communitarian moral thought.

Recently, Kevin Behrens (2013) and Anthony Oyowe (2018) have further distinguished between two distinct normative notions of personhood in the literature. Behrens talks of the *patient-centred* and *agent-centred* notions of personhood. Oyowe, on the other hand, talks of the *strongly* and *weakly normative* notions of personhood.[2] I believe these distinctions regarding the normative concepts of personhood are equivalent, and for the purposes of this book, I will use the more familiar distinction of the patient- and agent-centred notions of personhood. It is important to emphasise that both concepts are normative (or moral) in nature; however, they play different roles in moral discourse (see Behrens 2013; Molefe 2019a, Chapter 1). I turn now to a discussion of the patient-centred notion of personhood before proceeding to an analysis of the agent-centred notion.

The patient-centred notion of personhood is tantamount to the technical idea of *moral status* in moral philosophy. To say that some being has moral status means that its '… interests have some moral weight, independently of their effects on other beings who have moral status' (DeGrazia 2013, 25; see also 2008). Or, in the words of Anne Warren –

> To have moral status is to be morally considerable, or to have moral standing. It is to be an entity towards which moral agents have, or can have, moral obligations. If an entity has moral status, then we may not treat it in just any way we please; we are morally obliged to give weight in our deliberations to its needs, interests, or well-being. (1997, 4)

To attribute moral status to some entity is to pick it out as a being of intrinsic value. It is because this being is valuable in its own right that DeGrazia speaks of it as having independent moral weight and Warren refers to it as morally considerable. They do so to suggest that there are some facts about an entity with moral status (some needs, interests, or something about its wellbeing) that must be taken into consideration when we relate to it. In other words, to have moral status signifies being an entity of value whose presence creates moral obligations on the part of moral agents. Two crucial moral considerations arise from the idea of moral status. Firstly, to treat a being with moral status amiss is to violate a moral law. That is, a moral agent would have acted wrongly by doing so (Metz 2012a). Secondly, to treat a moral being amiss amounts to it being wronged or harmed. That is, the being would be made worse off insofar as its welfare, interests, needs or rights were undermined (Molefe 2017a).

Another way to make sense of the idea of moral status on the patient-centred notion of personhood is to invoke Stephen Darwall's (1977) notion of *recognition respect*. This refers to the respect owed to some entity in virtue of certain ontological properties it possesses. In other words, the respect imagined here tracks ontology. That is, we respect this particular entity for being the kind of a thing that it is or by focusing on those essential features of its ontological make-up crucial for it to function as the kind of a thing it is. For example, merely for the *fact* that someone is a president of a country, without regard to her performance in the office, we owe such an individual respect. It is the fact of the office she occupies that creates duties of respect for us as citizens of a country.

The idea of moral status attributes respect to some entity merely because it possesses relevant ontological features. Typically, in the literature, ontological features such as sentience, rationality, the soul, life, or basic capabilities have been invoked to generate different theories of moral status (see Bujo 2001; Iroegbu 2005; Singer 2009; Nussbaum 2011). These *relevant ontological features* are crucial because they are the ones that are central to the entity under consideration being able to lead a decent life. The reader should here appreciate the distinction between a *concept* and a *conception* of moral status. A concept of moral status is an abstract idea whose purpose is to identify beings of value — those that we owe recognition respect to. A conception of moral status is a theory that specifies the ontological feature(s) that determine beings of value, be it sentience, rationality or something else, in virtue of which the entity will be a member of the moral community (Metz 2012a, 2012b). In light of the above, we can conclude that the patient-centred notion of personhood is tantamount to the concept of moral status that identifies moral patients as those beings towards whom we expect to have moral obligations — obligations to honour their needs, interests, rights or wellbeing.

Apparently distinct to this is what Behrens identifies as the agent-centred notion of personhood. He associates the agent-centred notion of personhood with prominent scholars in African philosophy like Menkiti, Wiredu and Masolo. The essence of the agent-centred notion of personhood is that it refers to the moral *achievements* of the agent. To say of some moral agent that she is a person is to 'commend' or 'highly praise' her for the quality of her conduct or moral practice (Tutu 1999, 35; Wiredu 2009, 15). This idea of personhood captures the idea that the moral agent's deportment consistently reflects a morally virtuous character (Gyekye 1992, 2010). It tracks and reflects the quality of the *performance* of the moral agent against some standard of moral excellence (Presbey 2002; Eze 2018).

Another useful way to make sense of the idea of personhood is by employing Darwall's (1977) talk of *appraisal respect*. All of us may be presidents of different countries. Simply based on the fact that we are presidents, we are owed recognition respect by one another. Nevertheless, appraisal respect offers respect relative to the quality of the performance of each of us as agents (as presidents). The measure for the conduct of the agent is some standard of excellence. The better one performs as a president, the greater the respect one receives. The idea of appraisal respect is amenable to gradations, and one gets respect proportionate to how well or badly one performs as a president (Menkiti 2004; Wingo 2006). Some presidents will not get any respect at all, others will earn a small amount, and the outstanding ones will receive the most. The differentiating factor between these presidents is the quality of their performance in office. Personhood, understood in the light of appraisal respect, denotes the fact that moral agents will receive respect based on the consistent practice of moral excellence, which will manifest in a virtuous character. To say that one is a 'person' is to make the moral judgment that one is leading a genuinely human life; to deny one the appellation amounts to not approving of one's moral conduct.

It is important for the reader to notice that it is the agent-centred notion of personhood that is salient in the tradition of African philosophy. Scholars of African moral thought inform us that personhood is 'dominant', 'germane', 'the core of African traditional cultures', 'foundational and characteristic of African philosophical thought' and that it fills a 'central place…in African philosophy' (Ikuenobe 2006, 116 & 128; Wiredu 2009, 13; Behrens 2013, 104 & 105). Kwasi Wiredu informs us that Menkiti was the first to offer a philosophical elucidation of this concept in the tradition of African philosophy in the following quotation –

> In contemporary African philosophy the locus classicus of the normative conception of a person is Ifeanyi Menkiti's 'Person and Community in African Traditional Thought'…My own views are in substantial agreement with Menkiti's…Personhood…is something of an achievement.[3] (2004, 17)

In the light of the above, the reader will do well to remember that Menkiti (1984, 2004) penned two essays dedicated to the normative concept of personhood. The first essay is the one mentioned by Wiredu in the quotation above. The second essay (On the Normative Conception of a Person) is interested in the normative concept of personhood. Wiredu also specifies that the normativity in question is not property-based, as it is in the patient-centred notion of personhood; it is a performance-based concept under which personhood is construed as some kind of (moral) achievement.

It is also important to remember that Kwame Gyekye was initially highly critical of Menkiti's adumbrations of the idea of personhood in African philosophy (see Gyekye 1992, 105–10; see also Molefe 2019a, Chapter 2). But, Gyekye in his later restatement of the moral-political view of moderate communitarianism, is less critical of Menkiti's view of personhood; he opines that –

Introduction

> With all this said, however, this aspect of this [Menkiti's] account adumbrates a moral conception of personhood and is, on that score, interesting and relevant to the notion of personhood important for the communitarian framework. (1997, 64)

Here Gyekye endorses the relevance of the idea of personhood explicated by Menkiti in African philosophy. In the light of the above considerations, it is correct to conclude that the (agent-centred) normative idea of personhood is central to the tradition of African philosophy. We should also note that the defining essence of the idea of personhood in African philosophy is that it is conceived in terms of a moral process of achievement, usually captured in terms of a virtuous character (Eze 2018).

Several comments are crucial to consider regarding the distinction between the patient- and agent-centred notions of personhood. Firstly, Behrens informs us that they both draw a distinction between being human and being a person (2013, 103–104; see also Metz 2013a, 12). The fact of being human, though necessary for the attainment of personhood, does not guarantee it, in both senses of the term (Oyowe 2018).[4] Secondly, Behrens informs us that the patient-centred notion is more dominant in the Western moral tradition — specifically in bioethics and environmental ethics — whilst the agent-centred notion prevails in African philosophy (105; see Metz 2007, 331). Following the tendency in the literature of using these concepts separately, Oyowe (2018) repudiates the agent-centred notion — what he calls the strongly normative idea of personhood — and endorses the patient-centred notion of it.

The major strategy informing the present book is to appreciate the dual features of the idea of personhood as a moral theory — the patient-centred and agent-centred — that is often overlooked in the literature in African philosophy. The tendency is to focus only on the agent-centred facet of personhood. The proposal here is that a more robust approach to the ethics of personhood in African philosophy requires us to appreciate that the two concepts are interdependent. To illuminate the interdependence of these two moral concepts of personhood, I suggest that we recognise that the agent-centred notion of personhood is grounded on a particular view of the patient-centred notion — one that is usually implicit and not typically clarified, elaborated and defended in the literature. The idea here is that there is a certain ontological feature of being *human* (which informs the patient-centred notion) that is decisive for the very possibility of pursuing the agent-centred notion of personhood (see Molefe 2019a, Chapter 3). As a result, one of the outstanding features of this book is that it unfolds and articulates the patient-centred view of personhood (a theory of moral status/dignity that informs the agent-centred view) to pursue themes in applied ethics, a task that the agent-centred view alone cannot do.

As noted above, Behrens and Oyowe, in different ways and for different reasons, take these concepts to be distinct and diverging moral terms. In this book, however, I operate on the assumption of their moral interconnectedness and interdependence to articulate a more robust ethics of personhood in African philosophy. It is because human beings possess particular kinds of ontological features that we take them to be beings of value (having moral status, or dignity) and it is because of these same features that we can rightly expect them to pursue personhood (to lead morally virtuous lives).

Remember, this talk of the patient-centred notion of personhood is tantamount to talk of what constitutes moral status. It is this concept of moral status (dignity) that will be central to our approach to moral-political theorisation — an approach that will simultaneously recognise the importance of the agent-centred notion of personhood. In the next section, I discuss how I understand the idea of applied ethics.

What is applied ethics?

In this section, I explain my use and understanding of the idea of applied ethics. To illuminate the concept of applied ethics, it is crucial to differentiate among normative ethics, meta-ethics and applied ethics (see Pojman 2002). *Normative ethics* is concerned with specifying a general criterion [norm] of rightness of actions. Hedonistic utilitarianism, for example, as a moral theory stipulates the norm of pleasure, and based on this norm, distinguishes right from wrong actions (see Korsgaard 1983; Metz 2007). Right actions have a property of instantiating and maximizing pleasure and the wrong ones have the opposite effect (Kymlicka 1990). Normative theories can take a consequentialist, deontological and virtue-based framework (McNaughton and Rawling 2006). Meta-ethics is primarily concerned with fundamental questions assumed by (normative) ethics. Central to (normative) ethics are the concepts of right and wrong, and these are assumed obvious in normative theorisation. Meta-ethics will attempt either to give an account of such properties, or to deny that they exist (Mackie 1977; Pojman 2002). The property of rightness can be defined by appealing to the *subject* (ethical subjectivism), *culture* (cultural relativism), *God* (ethical supernaturalism), *nature* (ethical naturalism) (Sober 2001; Rachels and Rachels 2015). Ryberg, Peterson, and Wolf define applied ethics in this fashion –

> Applied ethics is a branch of ethics devoted to the treatment of moral problems, practices, and policies in personal life, professions, technology, and government…applied ethics takes its point of departure in practical normative challenges. (2007, 3)

Tom Beauchamp defines applied ethics as referring

> …to any use of philosophical methods to treat problems, practices, and policies in the professions, technology, government and the like. (2005, 3)

Two considerations stand out in these definitions of applied ethics. Firstly, both definitions affirm that applied ethics falls under the domain of ethics or moral philosophy. This explains why Beauchamp clarifies that applied ethics uses philosophical methods to pursue its tasks and aims. I understand philosophical methods to be constituted by two crucial facets, namely, conceptual analysis and argumentation (Dower 2008). Secondly, applied ethics focuses on problems related to personal life, professions, technology or governments. This second facet captures the practical or applied facet of ethics as it identifies or traces the emergence of moral issues in specific contexts of practice related to individuals or institutions or practical normative challenges. To appreciate better the second facet of this definition, consider for example the questions that emerge in bioethical contexts like stem cell research, abortion, suicide, the duties and responsibility of nurses, the importance of consent in medical practice, and so on. One can also consider questions that emerge in business ethics, like good leadership/management, responsible profit maximisation, and so on.

To address practical normative problems, I will draw from resources in African ethics, specifically, the idea of personhood. To address these problems, one could follow a monistic or pluralistic approach to the quest of imagining a unified account of disparate themes in applied ethics (Wolf 1999). This book will adopt a monistic approach. Thaddeus Metz (2012a, 67), in his discussion of human rights in African philosophy, identifies four salient grounding values in African moral thought — (1) life [vitality]; (2) dignity; (3) community; and (4) virtue [self-realisation]. Particularly in his intervention on the debate between radical and moderate communitarianism on the question of rights, Metz prescribes the value of *community* to be foundational, and proceeds to defend a view of rights based on this value (see Metz 2011, 2012b). For my part, I will invoke the ultimate value of *self-realisation* (personhood) and its underlying conception of dignity *qua* the capacity for sympathy to proffer a unified way to deal with practical moral problems in African philosophy.[5] In my view, it would be premature to espouse a pluralistic approach before we are able to demonstrate the inadequacy of a monistic one (see Metz 2013a). The kind of faith I manifest towards the possibility of a robust monistic theory is common in African moral philosophy.[6]

Before proceeding further, let me briefly reflect on two considerations. Firstly, the method I use to elucidate applied ethics. I will rely on the two facets of personhood as a moral view to articulate an African perspective on the practical problems that will be considered here, namely: *moral perfection* and *moral status/dignity*. Looked at from one angle, the ethics of personhood specifies the chief obligations of the agent to be her own moral perfection; and, looked at from another angle, it embodies standards that specify who is part of the moral community (moral status). Those who are part of the moral community are owed moral duties. Hence, the first and second chapters of this book are foundational insofar as they will philosophically unfold both dimensions of the ethics of personhood *qua* moral perfection and moral status (dignity). These two features of this moral theory will allow us to have a meaningful conversation about women, animals and development. For example, regarding the issues of animals, if it turns out that they have moral status then it follows that we have moral duties towards them.

Secondly, it is important that I clarify that this book makes a moderate promise. I do not imagine it as aiming to argue that the idea of personhood promises the most plausible view of discussing these applied ethics themes. Instead, it takes an expository posture insofar as it aims to articulate a personhood-based approach to questions related to the concept of dignity, the standing of women, the issue of animals and the concept of development. I think this kind of expository project is important for several reasons.

The first of these reasons is that this approach is an important development regarding the salient idea of personhood in African philosophy. It suggests one way to speak to Wiredu's (2009, 15) observation that the idea of personhood has a 'legion of implications' that are yet to be philosophically unfolded. This book offers one way to unfold the implications of personhood through explicating a conception of dignity inherent in this moral idea and further employing it to reflect on select applied ethics themes. Secondly, this book is important because it will be contributing an African perspective on values and issues that tend to be viewed through the prisms of Western culture(s), epistemology and axiology. The addition of an African perspective is good in its own right, as it speaks to the fact that Africans have their own way of understanding and relating to practical moral problems. Moreover, the addition of an African voice is crucial for two other projects. The first involves the call to decolonise knowledge in Africa, and many other parts of the world. The second involves creating a platform for dialogues between different cultures regarding these practical moral themes. An expository project of this kind is a useful starting point for promoting the decolonisation project and cross-cultural dialogue. Future works can then take a more comparative and argumentative posture.

Concepts and issues

I would now like to consider the status of the literature regarding the concepts and issues that are relevant in this book. First, I must make one clarificatory comment regarding my understanding of the ideas of ubuntu and personhood, and the relationship that I take to hold between them. This is important to address because I will draw extensively on the literature on ubuntu in the course of this book, and I would not want to leave the reader confused. I take the ideas of ubuntu and personhood to be continuous, if not synonymous. At least in this book, I stipulate the relationship to be as follows: I take the idea of ubuntu to be tantamount to the idea of personhood. That is, to say that someone has ubuntu is the same thing as to claim that they are a person or have achieved personhood. I take this position because the idea of ubuntu is essentially concerned with the idea of personhood — specifically, the agent-centred notion of it. This view is sustained by considering the aphorism that grounds ubuntu ethics.

Ubuntu, as an embodiment of an African moral view, is usually explained in terms of the following aphorism — 'A person is a person through other persons'. This aphorism does admit of *metaphysical* interpretations, where it specifies an account of personal identity in terms of human sociality or interdependence (Louw 2004). It is, however, the *moral* connotations of this aphorism that are of interest here. The reader will immediately realise that the idea of a *person* appears three times in the aphorism, but it is not immediately obvious which concepts of it are captured here (given that we have already specified at least four possible concepts of personhood in the literature).

The first reference to a person, in the aphorism above, is about the mere fact of being human — the *ontological* notion of personhood. The second instance of the word 'person' refers to the *normative* idea of personhood — the goal of morality prescribed by ubuntu ethics. The last instance of it, in the phrase 'through other persons', captures the importance of *social relationships* in the pursuit of personhood.[7] Put simply, the goal of morality according to the idea of ubuntu is for a human being to pursue a morally excellent character (this is, agent-centred personhood) and the only way to do so is through particular kinds of social relationships (Metz 2010a, 2010b; Molefe 2019a, 2019b). It becomes less surprising then that we are informed that 'the concept of ubuntu…is a statement about being, about fundamental things that qualify a person [human being] to be a person [morally virtuous]' (Dandala 2009, 260). In other words, those interpretations of ubuntu that construe it as embodying a self-realisation moral view are continuous with, or even equivalent to, the idea of personhood present in the works of leading scholars of African thought like Menkiti (1984, 2004); Gyekye (1992, 1997); Wiredu (1992, 2004); Ramose (1999); Masolo (2010); and Ikuenobe (2006, 2015, 2017).[8] It is equally important to recognise that any construal of ubuntu that does not take it to be a self-realisation view of morality will not necessarily be equivalent to the idea of personhood prevalent in African philosophy (see Matolino and Kwindingwi 2013; Praeg 2014; Etieyibo 2017).

With that clarified, we can consider the central idea of dignity in the literature in general and in African philosophy. The idea of dignity is an *essentially contested concept* (see Rodriguez 2015). The contested nature of this moral term could be understood in two ways, one extreme and the other heuristic. The view I have classified as 'extreme', is either overly critical of the idea of dignity or insists that we should repudiate this moral term altogether since it lacks conceptual clarity, or it is useless or it does not add any conceptual value (see Pinker 2008; Macklin 2003; Misztal, 2012). I must hasten, however, to add that this is not a dominant view in the literature. The second way of understanding the contested nature of the concept of dignity is to see the contestations not so much as being about the concept of dignity itself (at least not its validity) but about conflicting conceptions of it (see Metz 2012b; Formosa and Mackenzie 2014). In other words, scholars tend to agree on the validity of the concept of dignity and the value it embodies but differ on the specification of what constitutes it. It is this second approach to the idea of dignity *qua* personhood that will inform how this book will proceed. I will take the idea of dignity to be universally true, but I will proffer what I take to be an African conception of it by employing the idea of personhood (see Donnelly 1982).

The idea of dignity is usually deployed to refer to a property possessed by some entity (usually a human being) in virtue of which we owe it utmost moral respect (Darwall 1977). Jack Donnelly (2015, 1–2), one of the leading scholars of human rights, defines dignity to signify 'worth that demands recognition and respect. Those with dignity are due recognition as a result of possessing a particular honorable quality or status. They are also due the respect appropriate to that status or quality'. Put simply, to accord dignity to some being is to recognise it as possessing some ontological property that gives it a high status and objective moral worth. In virtue of this, we ought to respect the being in question. Normal adult human beings are taken to be paradigm examples of beings of dignity because they possess the morally relevant ontological features that assign them the honourable quality or status (DeGrazia 2008; Toscano 2011).

If this definition of dignity is right, then it has the following implications. Firstly, dignity is a property of an individual. In other words, the discourse of dignity (or, the dominant understanding of it) takes it to be *individualistic*. That is, dignity is a function of some property or characteristic of the individual (Molefe 2017b). Hence, it is common to read in the literature that dignity refers to 'worth that is *inherent*', or 'inalienable', or forming an 'inner, transcendental kernel' (Rosen 2012, 9; Miller 2017, 113; emphasis mine). The upshot of this view is that since dignity is a function of human nature, it is something that is not given and (in some sense) cannot be taken away, unless one's nature is fundamentally changed or destroyed (Miller 2017). One has it simply by being the kind of a thing one is.

Secondly, the idea of dignity is best characterised in *deontological* terms (see Toscano 2011; Rosen 2012). To elucidate the deontological nature of the idea of dignity, we can remember that there are two ways to relate to some value: one can either promote or honour it. Consequentialist accounts tend to promote a value, where the agent is required to maximise it or to make sure that there is as much of it as is possible in existence (McNaughton and Rawling, 1992). If one takes the value of love as an example, then the agent has a duty to make sure that there is as much of it in the world as is possible even if that can only be achieved through a few unloving acts (McNaughton and Rawling, 1992). But the deontological attitude of respecting a value is captured in this fashion – 'instead the idea is that a thing that has dignity ought to be honored in attitude and action'. This means that agents have a duty to respect such a being even when that attitude and its associated actions do not maximise the good, or even diminish it (McNaughton and Rawling, 1992). Put simply, the presence of beings of dignity demands unconditional respect.

Another facet related to the idea of dignity is that it offers one way to capture social egalitarianism. The idea of dignity accounted for in terms of some 'invariant' property of the individual is used to capture equality (Metz 2013a, 12). In this view, equality among individuals is a function of recognising some fact of their nature — the property that grounds their dignity (Darwall 1977). Individuals that possess the relevant property to a minimum threshold are equal and are owed equal moral regard. This is the case because dignity is not a function of achievement, but rather of merely possessing the relevant property.

It is important for the reader to notice that the scepticism that is sometimes expressed in the Western tradition towards the idea of dignity is generally absent in the literature of African philosophy. That is, African scholars are generally committed to the idea and ideals associated with the concept of dignity. Some scholars offer spiritual conceptions of dignity, where they ground it on the possession of life, or life force, or being part of a spiritual community (see Gyekye 1992; Bujo 2001; Ilesanmi 2001; Wiredu 1996a; Deng 2004; Iroegbu 2005; Bikopo and Van Bogaert 2009). These scholars take some divine feature of God, usually captured in terms of vitality, or *okra* — spiritual energy — as the basis for dignity (Wiredu 1996; Deng 2004; Imafidon 2013; Molefe 2018). On the other hand, you find scholars that take a secular approach to dignity, where they account for it by appeal to some *natural* property. Some scholars ground it on the human capacity for autonomy, or the relational capacity for care, or the capacity to enter into particular kinds of social relationships (see Gyekye 1997; Ramose 2009; Metz 2012b). For my part, I will stipulate a secular interpretation of dignity.

Recently, Polycarp Ikuenobe (2017, 2018), one of the leading scholars of personhood, provides his own version of a personhood-based view of dignity. He refuses to ground dignity, as is typically done in moral philosophy, on the mere possession of some ontological feature. Ikuenobe argues instead that a plausible African view of dignity ought to account for it in terms of how the agent uses her ontological features to attain personhood (moral excellence). He considers the possession of some ontological property to be merely instrumentally good, which means that dignity emerges as a result of how the agent uses it. In this book, I will propose an alternative conception of dignity *qua* personhood that grounds it on the mere possession of the capacity for virtue after raising serious objections against Ikuenobe's performance-based view of dignity. I do so motivated by two considerations. Firstly, I believe that our pioneers of the idea of personhood — Menkiti and Gyekye — anticipated that it embodies a conception of dignity (even though they never went on to articulate it fully and apply it to various practical moral problems) (see Menkiti 1984, 171; Gyekye 1992, 109–10). Secondly, I believe that this conception is robust enough to offer under-explored insights and perspectives on various moral-political [applied ethics] concepts.

Now let us consider the literature regarding the status of women in African philosophy. Scholars of African cultures decry and criticise them for their tendency to treat women as secondary citizens. The social order of African societies tends to revolve around men (see Walker 2013). This criticism finds its most recent expressions, specifically as it relates to the idea of personhood, in the writings of Anthony Oyowe (2013), Oyowe and Olga Yurkivska (2014), Kai Horsthemke (2018), Nompumelelo Manzini (2018) and Elvis Imafidon (2019). These scholars argue that the idea of personhood is essentially inegalitarian insofar as it embodies a conception of social relations that is gendered, and in which the roles associated with men are considered superior and those assigned to women inferior. Horsthemke (2018) argues that the idea of personhood is in some respects too wide and in others too narrow. Personhood is too wide insofar as it includes ancestors as part of the moral community; and it is too narrow insofar as it excludes foetuses, children, women, homosexuals and animals, among others. In this book, I will evaluate the plausibility of the accusation that the idea of personhood excludes women from the moral community. I will also be considering whether the idea of personhood can, alternatively, embody a plausible gender-neutral and egalitarian social vision.

Next, I would like to consider the question of the moral place of animals in our societies — a question which is gaining traction in African philosophy. Recently, we have seen a rise in doctoral theses arguing that African ethics is open to non-anthropocentric interpretations, which grant animals some moral status (see Behrens 2011; Chemhuru 2016). Kai Horsthemke (2015, 2017, 2018) has insisted that ubuntu/personhood ethics or personhood is intrinsically anthropocentric, and hence fails to proffer a plausible moral view. Scholars such as Behrens (2010), Metz (2012), Chemhuru (2016 2018) and Etieyibo (2017) have pointed to the fact that African moral thought does embody a robust animal ethics, a view that Horsthemke (2017) contests. For my part, I will limit myself to considering whether the view of personhood can embody a promising animal ethics. The pioneers of personhood, Menkiti and Gyekye, suggest this view implies that animals have no moral status at all. I will propose a reading of their work that suggests otherwise, which will imply that we have moral duties to animals.

And finally, let us turn to the theme of development. It is crucial to appreciate that the idea of development is an essentially contested notion. There is no single definition and approach to the discourse in which there is convergence or agreement. In fact, some scholars in the African tradition insist that we should abandon this discourse altogether since it is a concept that is reflective and reproductive of the hegemony and exploitative tendencies of the West (Fine 2009; Metz 2017). Some scholars, however, propose approaches to the discourse on development that are based on value systems indigenous in African cultures (see Kudadjie 1992; Dei 1993, 2000; Segage 2018). Some scholars appeal to the spiritual value of vitality (Bujo 2001; Ajei 2007), others point to the ideals embodied in Pan Africanism as found in the writings and experiments of Kwame Nkrumah or Julius Nyerere (Wiredu 2008; Segage 2018), others point us to the history of development in Africa as a basis to draw inspiration and theorise development (Keita 2004).

In this book, I adopt a framework proposed in the development ethics discourse (see Goulet 1996; Dower 2008). I will then draw from the indigenous value system inherent in the discourse on personhood to construct an African account of development in the light of the conceptual framework proposed in the discourse of development ethics. In the final analysis, I will point out that development revolves around providing socio-political and political conditions conducive for individuals to pursue personhood.

Structure of the book

This book has five chapters and a conclusion. The first chapter discusses personhood as a moral theory. It examines the agent-centred facet of personhood, focusing on personhood as a moral theory *qua* moral perfectionism. The second chapter explicates the patient-centred facet of personhood as a moral theory. In it, the focus is on philosophically unfolding the conception of moral status or dignity inherent in the discourse of personhood. The third chapter looks at the question of women in the light of the idea of personhood. The fourth chapter considers the status of animals in African philosophy; and the final chapter investigates the topic of development in the light of personhood.

I draw the attention of the reader to the following considerations. Parts of the material in chapters one and five appears in some of my published articles. This book is a result of the research I have been doing on the idea of personhood (see Molefe 2016, 2017b, 2018, 2019a, 2019c). I also advise the reader that these chapters were written largely independently of one another. This will explain why the same, very few, quotations will feature in different chapters. The quotations that feature repeatedly in different chapters are those associated with Menkiti and Gyekye, particularly when articulating their conceptions of dignity. These quotations and the theoretical improvements I made on them form the substance of the idea of dignity that is central in this book, and hence warrant their repetition. I hope the reader will indulge me.

Conclusion

To conclude, I bring one final consideration to the attention of the reader. This book operates on a particular meta-ethical assumption. One could approach moral theorisation on secular or religious grounds (see Molefe 2015a, 2015b). That is, one could invoke natural (ethical-naturalism) or spiritual (ethical-supernaturalism) properties as the normative bases of moral theorisation. In this book, I stipulate ethical naturalism as the best way to approach moral-political philosophy. I do so for two reasons. Firstly, the dominant view in the literature in African philosophy seems to endorse a secular approach rather than a religious one as the most plausible way to construe African moral thought (see Wiredu 1980; Gyekye 1995, 2010; Okeja 2013). This is by no means to reject the possibility of religiously oriented approaches to applied ethics. Instead, it is to pursue a unified account of African moral thought based on non-controversial metaphysical considerations, which I believe will appeal to those with a secular bent. I believe this to be a fruitful way of articulating a plausible theory and providing a useful comparison with other secular traditions of philosophy.

In the next chapter, I articulate the ethics of personhood *qua* moral perfection and moral status.

Notes

1   The above point regarding going beyond the fixation on rights in the light of personhood makes sense when one considers the literature on African philosophy. A careful consideration of the literature reveals that scholars of African moral and political thought, particularly those committed to the idea of personhood, have largely been fixated on the idea of rights (see Menkiti 1984; Gyekye 1992, 1997; Wiredu 1996a; Matolino 2009, 2014; Famanikwa 2010; Oyowe 2014a, 2014b; Molefe 2016, 2018, 2019a; Chemhuru 2018a; Ikuenobe 2018). This book is one attempt to extend conversations on personhood beyond the fixation on rights, and to imagine other under-explored crucial moral-political concepts.

2   Oyowe (2018) believes that the strongly normative view is implausible for a variety of reasons, one of which is that it fails to embody an egalitarian political theory. I hope to demonstrate otherwise by providing a more plausible understanding of personhood in this book.

3   Two points are crucial to keep in mind regarding the history of the concept of personhood. Firstly, Wiredu's comment should be correctly interpreted to mean that Menkiti was the first to explicitly offer a systematic exposition of the idea of personhood

Introduction

in the tradition of African philosophy. This way of reading matters is consistent with the fact that the idea was already anticipated and implicit in discussions by Tempels (1959) and Mbiti (1969), among others. Secondly, it is also interesting to notice that Wiredu informs us that anthropologists had also observed this idea among African cultures (see Wiredu 2004, 2009).

4   Though a human infant or a foetus may be a human being, she is not a person in terms of the agent-centred notion and (in some interpretations) she may also not be a person in terms of the patient-centred notion.

5   Talk of self-realisation as the basic value underscores the fact that the ethics of personhood (or at least one facet of it) requires the agent to perfect herself — that is, to become the best she can be, morally speaking (Menkiti 1984; Wiredu 2009; Shutte 2001). There are other expressions to capture this facet of the ethics of personhood, such as *autocentrism* (Van Niekerk 2007), *moral perfection* (Behrens 2013), and *moral virtue* (Gyekye 1992, 2010).

6   The reader will note that scholars like Wiredu (1992), Bujo (2001), Gyekye (2004);,Metz (2007) and Van Niekerk (2007) espouse ethical monism of one form or another.

7   In this particular discussion, it is not important at this stage that I be specific about the exact role played by social relationships in the discourse of personhood. It suffices for now to state that social relationships could either play a constitutive or instrumental role. Thaddeus Metz (2013b) defends the view that certain social relationships constitute personhood. I defend the view that social relationships, at best, play an instrumental role (see Molefe 2019b).

8   These scholars never use the idea of ubuntu in their elucidations of the idea of personhood.

1

Personhood as a moral theory

Introduction

The aim of this chapter is to proffer an interpretation of personhood as a moral theory. I will articulate personhood as an agent-centred theory of value — an African theory of virtue. As an agent-centred theory of value, I will argue that personhood embodies a perfectionist moral view that enjoins the agent to realise her true humanity. I start by discussing the agent-centred facet of personhood as a moral theory, as opposed to the patient-centred one, for two reasons. Firstly, I do so because it tends to feature significantly in the literature in African philosophy (see Menkiti 1984; Gyekye 1992; Wiredu 2009; Ikuenobe 2016; Oyowe 2018). It will be crucial, therefore, for me to be clear regarding how I construe personhood as a moral theory. Secondly, I do so because this discussion will lay the foundation for the next chapter on dignity, which will be pivotal for the rest of the book. I believe the exposition of personhood as a theory of virtue is important insofar as it is one side of the coin of the ethics of personhood.

To articulate the agent-centred theory of value associated with personhood, I structure this chapter as follows. I will first draw a distinction between being human and being a person. Secondly, I will consider the content of what it means to be a person in the moral sense. I will submit that personhood embodies a perfectionist moral theory. I will then proceed to consider four moral considerations associated with the perfectionist theory of morality *qua* personhood, namely: (1) the character-focused nature of morality; (2) the moral individualism inherent in it; (3) its egoism; and (4) the place and role it assigns to social relationships. I will proceed to articulate how this theory accounts for the rightness of actions. Finally, I will conclude by considering two criticisms of the moral theory that I put forward.

I advise the reader to remember that this chapter is not predicated on the assumption that the idea of personhood promises the most plausible moral view.

It is based, rather, on a humble exploratory and expository approach, where I aim to share the moral-theoretical content, and the consequences, of taking the idea of personhood seriously in African moral philosophy.

Personhood as an agent-centred theory of value[1]

The aphorism definitive of ubuntu ethics — 'a person is a person through other persons' — is generally understood by cultural practitioners and scholars to embody an African moral worldview. It brings to mind three distinct facets that constitute an African moral view, namely: (1) the fact of being human as the basis for morality; (2) the essence and goal of morality; and (3) the essential role of social relationships in the pursuit of the moral goal. Below, I explicate personhood as a moral theory by elaborating (1) and (2) and I will come back to (3) when I consider implications of (2).

The first reference to personhood in the aphorism points to the fact of being human — what in the literature is captured as the ontological notion of personhood (see Oyowe 2014a; Ikuenobe 2006, 2016). Scholars of African moral thought have, in several ways, brought to our attention that morality in the discourse of personhood is predicated on some distinctive features of human nature. This comment by Ramose in Bewaji and Ramose is informative –

> *...the concept of a person in African thought takes the fact of being a human being for granted.* It is assumed that one cannot discuss the concept of personhood without in the first place admitting the 'human existence' of the human being upon whom personhood is to be conferred.[2] (2003, 413; emphasis mine)

This comment by Ramose makes sense when interpreted in the light of the distinction between the ontological and normative concepts of personhood in African philosophy (Wiredu 1996a; Behrens 2013; Ikuenobe, 2016). The ontological notion refers to the fact of being human, what Ramose refers to above as 'human existence', constituted by certain descriptive features such as having a body, and so on (Kaphagawani 2004). The normative notion refers to the reflexive process of moral becoming, where the agent adds dimensions of moral virtue to her own humanity (Eze 2018; Menkiti 2018). Understood in the light of this distinction, the comment by Ramose may be construed as making the point that the moral discourse of personhood takes the fact of being human as a point of departure, at least some crucial features of it are necessary for the possibility of moral-becoming. This point is put more appositely by Oyowe (2018, 784) when he states that the fact of being human is a necessary but insufficient condition for personhood. In other words, certain facts of human nature are required for human beings to be able to pursue personhood. It is also crucial to notice that these ontological facts, in and of themselves, do not constitute personhood — something else is required for personhood to emerge.

The reader may here wonder about the ontological considerations that inform the moral discourse of personhood. Let me highlight three of these. Firstly, scholars of African metaphysical and moral thought tend to conceive of human nature in a positive light. In other words, human beings are not considered to come into the world with a warped or corrupted nature (see Gyekye 1995, 2010). When human beings come into the world, they emerge as morally neutral beings. Moral corruption or guilt is entirely a function of human agency. A human being comes into the world with a nature that can go either way in terms of moral conduct. The direction is dictated almost entirely by the decisions and conduct of the agent. This view of human nature is completely at odds with the Catholic view of original sin or the idea that human beings have a fallen nature (Gyekye 2010). The African view of human nature associated with personhood is also at odds with the view of human nature that is associated with the idea of the state of nature — psychological egoism. That metaphysical view understands human nature to be essentially selfish, which tends to serve as a metaphysical grounding for the idea of the state of nature (see Wolf 1999).

Secondly, in the discourse of personhood, human nature and human personality are conceptualised in relational terms. Human nature is understood to be wired for social relationships. This idea is well captured by John Mbiti's (1969) famous assertion that — 'I am because we are'. Here, the dominant view is to make sense of human existence, socialisation and personal identity in terms of social relationships. Menkiti's comment regarding this maxim by Mbiti is illuminating –

> Its sense is not that of a person [human being] speaking on behalf of, or in reference to, another, but rather of an individual, *who recognizes the sources of his or her own humanity*, and so realises, with internal assurance, that in the absence of others, no grounds exist for a claim regarding the individual's own standing as a person. (2004, 324; emphasis mine)

The crucial point to notice is that one's status as a human being traces its source to social relationships with others. Without social relationships with others, the very project of being human is put in jeopardy. It should therefore not come as a surprise when Tutu (1999, 35) avers that 'my humanity is caught up, [it] is inextricably bound up in yours'. The metaphysical view propounded here is that one cannot imagine one's humanity apart from social relations with other human beings (see Dandala 2009; Mothlabi and Munyaka 2009). A plausible metaphysical view embodied in the discourse of personhood is that we should recognise that we experience our humanity in terms of being-with-others (Louw 2004). This point is accentuated by Gyekye (1992, 104) when he notes that 'the fundamentally relational character of the person [human being] and the interdependence of human individuals arising out of their *natural sociality* are thus clear'. The idea here is that we should appreciate the social nature of being human. In other words, the high value placed on the group in African cultures and in African socio-moral theorisation is an outgrowth of a particular philosophical anthropology, one where human beings are conceived of as beings designed for and wired to function and thrive in social relationships (see Paris 1995; Mbigi 2005).

We now come close to that feature of human nature that makes personhood possible. Before we get to that feature, we must first note that human nature is believed to have the capacity to grow or diminish morally. This point is captured as follows by Sebidi –

> For Africans, human nature is capable of increasing or decreasing almost to a point of total extinction. There are actions…that are conducive to the enhancement or growth of a person's nature, just as there are those which are destructive of a person's nature. (1988, 48)

Here we see the crucial point that human nature is conceived in terms of its capacity to morally grow or deteriorate. In other words, in our nature we are wired with capacities that make us susceptible to morality or, more specifically, to pursuing and achieving personhood. It is for this reason that Gyekye (1992, 109) is correct to assert that 'much is expected of a person (human being) in terms of the display of moral virtue [achieving personhood]' in African moral cultures. For Gyekye, this moral expectation for human beings to pursue and possibly achieve personhood [moral virtue] is grounded on his conception of human nature, which is that 'the practice of moral virtue is *intrinsic* to the conception of person' (1992, 109; emphasis mine). There is a metaphysical view that informs the moral expectation for a human being to be able to achieve the status of personhood. To say that the practice of virtue is intrinsic to the conception of personhood [human nature] should [plausibly] be construed to mean that human beings have the ontological faculties required to lead morally virtuous lives, and not [implausibly] that it is automatic and guaranteed that human beings will lead virtuous lives (see Gyekye 2010 – the section in the entry titled: 'Moral Personhood'). I will be more specific regarding the intrinsic capacities that make the pursuit of personhood possible in the next chapter, where I will elucidate the conception of dignity associated with the idea of personhood.

In the light of these adumbrations on the fact of being human, we come to the following observations. Human beings come into the world without the burden of inheriting the sins [moral liabilities] of their forebears. They come guilt-and-praise free. They come with a nature teeming with moral possibilities and, all things being equal, the agent is ultimately responsible for her own moral destiny, whether it will be a moral success or failure (Wingo 2006). Her moral destiny is in her own hands because she has the ontological capacities and features that make personhood possible.

We need to proceed to consider the second reference to personhood in the aphorism — remember, 'a person is a *person*…' The second instance of personhood refers to the *moral goal* posited by ubuntu as a moral view. The goal of morality is to convert the moral possibilities of human nature into moral reality by 'decorating' one's humanity with moral excellence. Menkiti's thoughts in this regard are informative –

> We must also conceive of this [human] organism as going through a long process of social and ritual transformation until it attains the full complement of excellencies seen as truly definitive of man. (1984, 172)

Here we are informed that the pursuit of personhood is a socio-moral process of transformation, where the agent pursues, espouses, and ultimately exhibits moral excellence. It is crucial to notice that the idea being considered here is normative insofar as Menkiti talks of excellencies *seen as truly definitive of a man*. The idea of personhood refers to a moral state attained by human beings that are leading genuine human lives (see Metz 2010, 83). Notice that Menkiti refers to the acquisition of personhood as a long process. This is because it takes a long time to morally actualise raw human capacities to reach a point where they are characterised by excellence (Wiredu 2009). The aim of this process is to lead to 'ethical maturity' or a 'widened maturity of ethical sense' (Menkiti 2004, 325; 2018, 165). To achieve moral maturity the agent must be consistently engaged in the process of moral 'self-creation' or the 'ingathering of the (moral) excellencies' (Menkiti 1984, 172; Agada and Egbai 2018, 149).

In this light, to call someone a person is to make a moral judgement about the quality of their character. It is to judge the moral agent's character to be characterised by 'moral practice' or even moral 'excellence' (Menkiti 1984, 172; Gyekye 1992, 113). It is also crucial to notice that the language used by scholars of African thought in speaking of personhood is that of *virtue*, which signals the idea of character (see Van Niekerk 2007, 2013). For example, Tutu (1999, 35) associates ubuntu with the virtues of kindness, friendliness, compassion, sharing and so on. More or less the same list of virtues can be seen in Wiredu (1992); Gyekye (1992); and Mokgoro (1998). It is important to notice that the virtues associated with ubuntu/personhood in this grab-bag list of virtues are exclusively relational by nature. In other words, these are other-regarding virtues, which embody duties and responsibilities, with almost no explicit mention of self-regarding virtues or duties (see Metz 2012a). Hence, we note that a human being characterised by personhood is one that relates positively to others. This *positive relation* to others takes place in the context of the consistent instantiation of the other-regarding virtues.

From the above, it emerges that the idea of personhood presupposes a particular kind of moral theory. Wiredu captures this insight thus –

> But such evaluation [that one is a person or a non-person] presupposes a system of values. Since the context of such evaluations is nothing short of the entire sphere of human relations, the system of values presupposed cannot be anything short of an ethic… (2009, 15)

Here, Wiredu informs us that personhood embodies a particular system of values, or an ethical perspective. Gyekye (2010) also informs us that 'the concept of a person in African thought embodies ethical presuppositions'. It is unfortunate, however, that these scholars do not go further to specify the kind of approach to morality that is presupposed by the idea of personhood. Wiredu does at least inform us that the system of value imagined here is meant to regulate all forms of social relations. If this system of value is so pervasive that it affects every sphere of human existence, it is urgent that we be clear regarding its specific nature. Behrens makes the following commentary regarding the nature of the moral system embodied by personhood –

> Menkiti's association of the term 'excellencies' with personhood also implies that becoming a person is essentially related to developing virtue. Thus, *the African conception of personhood could be thought to propose a theory of ethics that brings to mind what Western philosophy calls 'perfectionism'*… (2013, 111; emphasis mine)

Behrens is contrasting the notion of personhood salient in African philosophy, the agent-centred notion, with the one dominant in Western philosophy, the patient-centred notion. He associates this idea of personhood with leading scholars of African thought like Menkiti, Wiredu and Masolo. As captured in the quotation above, Behrens' analysis notes that African scholars tend to associate personhood with moral excellence or a virtuous character. This accords with what was discussed above. In this light, it is safe to observe that personhood imagines a transformational process where raw capacities of human nature are converted into bearers of moral virtue. As a result, we can endorse the view that the moral idea of personhood embodies a perfectionist moral theory, where the agent is required to perfect her own human humanity. The perfection imagined here has to do with character perfection or human excellence, and the ideal character is one that exudes other-regarding virtues like generosity, kindness, friendliness, forgiveness, lovingness and so on (see Tutu 1999; Mokgoro 1998). In the next section, I consider some implications of understanding personhood as a perfectionist moral theory.

Implications of the agent-centred theory of value

Above, we did an exposition of personhood as a moral theory by elaborating the aphorism of Ubuntu — a person is a person through other persons — that captures one salient way to approach African moral thought. Our analysis of personhood as

moral theory in light of the aphorism of personhood has thus far only covered the first two references to the idea of personhood — the ontological notion and normative one. In pursuing the implications that flow from the normative idea of personhood, we will also consider the last part of the aphorism — through other persons — that captures the role and place of social relationships in the discourse of ubuntu, or the pursuit of personhood *qua* moral excellence. Below, I consider four implications of the agent-centred theory of value embodied by personhood, namely: (1) the agent-centred approach to morality; (2) moral individualism; (3) moral egoism; and (4) the role of social relationships.

1. The agent-centred approach to morality

Typically, modern moral theories tend to focus on *action* (see Pojman 2002). The aim of modern theorisation is to posit some norm as the basis of right and wrong action. For example, utilitarianism accounts for rightness and wrongness of actions by appeal to the norm of utility, be it construed in terms of pleasure or informed preferences (Kymlicka 1990). The idea of personhood, as we have observed above, and in contrast, makes its primary focus the *agent* herself. The focus of morality in the discourse of personhood revolves around the kind of a human being the moral agent ought to become.

In this light, we can rightly distinguish between action-centred and agent-centred moral theories (Annas 1992). This distinction is rough, but it helps us understand personhood as a moral theory. In this view, it is not that actions do not count (as the reader will see below), but that that they count insofar as they reflexively contribute to, emanate from, and reflect the quality of character of the agent. This understanding of morality is expressed thus by Gyekye (2010) –

> Thus, the inquiries into the moral language of several African peoples or cultures indicate that in these languages the word or expression that means 'character' is used to refer to what others call 'ethics' or 'morality'. Discourses or statements about morality turn out to be discourses or statements essentially about character… The implication here is that ethics or morality is conceived in terms essentially of character.

Here, Gyekye considers the language used by some African cultures in referring to morality and ethics. He concludes that the words or concepts used to refer to morality within these cultures are essentially character-based. I submit that this is also the case regarding the idea of personhood. The reason for this view is captured thus by Menkiti (1984, 171) when he states that the '…word "muntu" includes an idea of excellence, of plenitude of force at maturation…' The Nguni word 'umu-ntu', or the equivalent Sotho word 'mo-tho', can be translated as 'person'. It has both the ontological and normative references contained in the translated word (see Ramose 1999; LenkaBula 2008). It is the normative reference of *muntu* that Menkiti associates with moral excellence or maturation in this context (see Behrens 2013). It is also important to consider the fact that Menkiti (1984) associates personhood with the idea of (moral) excellence four times. In one instance, he makes the following comment — '…so that what was initially biologically given can come to attain social self-hood, i.e., become a person with all the inbuilt excellencies implied by the term' (172). Menkiti informs us that the term 'personhood' implies moral excellence — or has the idea of moral excellence built into it. Thus, to ascribe personhood to some moral agent is tantamount to moral approbation. The ascription morally judges her as manifesting moral habits consistent with moral excellence.

From the above, I believe that it is clear that the idea of personhood as a moral theory embodies a character-based morality, which makes the agent the focus of morality insofar as she has the duty to pursue moral perfection.

2. Moral individualism

In several of my previously published pieces of research, I argue for the view outlined in what follows (see Molefe 2017b, 2019a, 2019b). I do not use the idea of individualism in a pejorative sense to criticise an individual or culture for being selfish or self-centred. I use it in the sense employed in the context of environmental ethics instead, where we distinguish between individualism, holism and relationalism in our approaches to account for moral status (see Behrens 2010; May 2014; Metz 2012b; Molefe 2017a, b, 2019b). To claim that a theory is 'individualistic' is to observe that it locates morality in some internal property of the agent — such as rationality, interest, desire and so on (May 2014). It is crucial to notice that the idea of personhood makes some facet of human nature the basis for morality. The individual is morally required to perfect her own humanity. In other words, there is an intrinsic feature of human nature that the moral agent must develop or nurture for her to attain the status of a moral exemplar.

The individualism of personhood is best captured by the fact that the idea of personhood is character-centred. The idea that personhood is individualistic is noted by Metz in his analysis of salient theories of African moral thought (where one of the theories he considers is that of personhood). In this regard (and regarding other African moral theories), Metz (2007, 331; emphasis mine) makes the following comment — 'Notice that the above four [theories] ground morality in something *internal to the individual*, whether it be her life (U1), well-being (U2), rights (U3), or self-realisation (U4).' I advise the reader to note that Metz uses the phrase 'self-realisation' to refer to personhood (Metz 2007, 330–331; see also Wood 2007; Molefe 2019b). I hope the point is clear that the idea of personhood makes some facet of the individual the entire focus of morality. The moral process focuses on the character of the agent and the goal is the perfection of that character.

3. Moral egoism

One of the crucial questions we need to clarify to get a better understanding of personhood as a perfectionist moral theory is whether it should be understood in egoist or non-egoist terms. Roughly, the major difference between egoistic and non-egoistic perfectionist interpretations is that the former posits the pursuit of personhood as being the sole responsibility of the agent herself, while the latter extends our duty to include even the perfection of others (see Wall 2012). It is my considered view that the correct interpretation of the perfectionism associated with personhood is of the egoistic type (see Molefe 2019a, Chapter 3). This view is justified by the fact that scholars of personhood talk of it in a way that suggests moral egoism. Augustine Shutte supports the idea that egoism is the appropriate interpretation, in this fashion –

> The moral life is seen as a process of *personal growth*…Our deepest moral obligation is to become more fully human. (2001, 30; emphasis mine)

Metz also notes that –

> The ultimate goal of a person, self, or human in the biological sense should be to become a *full* person, a *real* self, or a *genuine* human being, i.e., to exhibit virtue in a way that not everyone ends up doing. (2010, 83; emphasis mine)

The egoistic view of personhood is further corroborated by Menkiti (2018, 165) — 'My answer here is that God may have created us, but we have to make ourselves into the persons that God wanted us to be'. We can understand Menkiti as drawing a distinction between human ontological completeness and moral incompleteness. As creations of God, we naturally grow into human beings. But the project of personhood involves pursuing and fulfilling moral completeness. God leaves the project of completing ourselves morally in our hands to pursue the destiny of our human nature. Menkiti cautions us that the project of moral completion should not be construed such that its aim is to replace 'God as the author of our being, but rather that our being as persons in the world is substantially of our making' (2018, 166). The point is clear — as human beings we are created with certain moral potentialities, but it is the task of each agent to ultimately pursue her own moral self-perfection.

To hold an egoistic view is not tantamount to the idea that we may not assist or relate to others as they pursue their own perfection. The egoistic view only insists that the perfection of each individual is ultimately her own responsibility. The community or social structures one inhabits ought to create enabling conditions for moral agents, but these are not sufficient for the possibility of moral perfection. Moral perfection must flow from the agent's own efforts to make herself morally appreciable (Gyekye 1997).

I believe that the non-egoistic view is implausible and indeed I consider it to be seriously misguided. This is the case insofar as it imposes '…that each human being has a non-derivative duty to perfect others as well as a duty to perfect himself' (Wall 2012; see also Molefe 2019a, Chapter 3). It is reasonable to impose on each agent the responsibility to perfect herself. To extend the responsibility of perfection towards others, however, seems to be misguided since we can only do so much for them in the moral sphere. We can encourage, admonish, or reprimand them, and so on. Only the agent herself, however, can close the bridge between moral knowledge and moral action. It seems reasonable to leave the specific responsibility of pursuing moral perfection, ultimately, in the hands of each individual since only the individual can activate and nurture her own moral dispositions. To impose this duty on other moral agents (as the non-egoistic interpretation of personhood would do) is to overlook 'that there are serious limits to our ability to bring about the perfection of others' (Wall 2012, n.p.). To appreciate these serious limits requires that we come to terms with the fact that we have no control over agential facets that are necessary for moral action and perfection, such as intention, desire, will-power, moral decision, moral actions and so on, which can only be controlled by the agent herself. If there is a moral sphere that is entirely within the locus of control of the agent when it comes to moral action and the pursuit of moral perfection, then it seems reasonable to limit the responsibility for personal perfection to the agent herself.

The final implication of the agent-centred theory of value relates to the role of social relationships in the discourse of personhood, and I turn to it next.

4. Social relationships in personhood

One of the defining features of African moral thought is the high value it places on groups or the concept of community (Gyekye 1992; Paris 1995; Mbigi 2005). Scholars of African moral thought generally take social relationships to play a crucial role in the discourse of personhood. However, it is not entirely clear whether relationships play a *causal* or *constitutive* role in the discourse of personhood (see Metz 2013a; Tshivhase 2013). I take social relationships to play an *instrumental* role. I have already elaborated this view in other places in my research; I will not defend it here (see Molefe, 2017b, 2019a, Chapter 3; 2019b). I believe this quotation from Menkiti (1984, 172; emphasis mine) will suffice for now to secure the instrumental role of social relationships — '…during this long process of attainment [of personhood], the community plays a vital role as *catalyst* and as *prescriber* of norms.' The two terms employed by Menkiti lead to the view that the idea of personhood plays an instrumental role in pursuing it. A *catalyst* (a term borrowed from chemistry) serves as a *means* in the chemical process and never as an end; it accelerates and enhances the process, but it is not part of the final product. The idea that the community also serves as the *prescriber* of norms implies that social relationships and institutions serve as moral guides; it is ultimately the moral agent that ought to internalise and actualise the prescribed values of excellence as a feature of her own moral existence (Ikuenobe 2015).

Above, we noted four implications flowing from the moral perfectionist interpretation of personhood as a moral theory. We noted the agent-centred nature of this moral view, where the focus is on the status of virtue which the agent ought to attain. Then we considered the individualistic nature of this moral view insofar as the good is a function of some facet of the individual — specifically the character of the agent. We proceeded to discuss the egoistic nature of this moral view. And, finally, we noted the instrumentality of social relationships in the moral agent's quest to pursue and attain personhood.

Personhood as a principle of right action

To seal the above discussion of the implications of personhood as a moral theory, I offer a rendition of it as an action-centred theory of value.[3] This will make the theory more accessible and useful given that the development of character requires, in the first instance, the habitual performance of right actions. This view is captured in this fashion by Gyekye (2010) — 'A person is therefore responsible for the state of his or her character, for character results from the habitual actions of a person', which produces 'excellences of character'. If one were to pursue personhood, surely one ought to be able to specify what actions count as right and wrong, or serve as essential building blocks for moral perfection? In other words, a robust agent-centred theory requires a 'decision-making procedure' for distinguishing acts that lead to virtue from those that lead to moral corruption (Annas 1992, 129). This should not be read as contradicting what is stated above regarding the agent-centredness of this moral view. It should instead be understood to be augmenting it by specifying the building blocks of what constitute a virtuous character — namely actions that lead to moral habit formation, and that ultimately result in a sound character (see Gyekye 2010). To articulate an action-centred theory associated with personhood, I draw from Metz, who reduces personhood to this theory of right action –

> An action is right just insofar as it positively relates to others and thereby realises oneself; an act is wrong to the extent that it does not perfect one's valuable nature as a social being. (2007, 330)

This principle accounts for right action by specifying two crucial considerations.

Firstly, right actions are characterised by the property of contributing to the agent ultimately realising her true self, i.e. an acquisition of a virtuous character. In other words, the consistent performance of right action leads to moral habituation, which results in the production of moral perfection. Secondly, this principle also specifies the means the agent ought to use to realise her true humanity — namely by relating positively to others. The goal of morality, in this view, is the perfection of the self, which manifests in the agent's disposition to exude moral virtues in the context of relating positively to others.

To demonstrate the robustness of this principle of right action, we can consider how it accounts for the case of rape. According to Kant's Formula of Humanity, rape is wrong because it treats the woman merely as a means. The act of rape fundamentally violates her 'humanity' — that is, her capacity for rational and autonomous action as a self-governing entity. In a fundamental sense, rape objectifies and instrumentalises the woman's humanity and body for the pleasure of the perpetrator. The woman is reduced to a mere provider of pleasure. In the light of personhood, however, a different reason is given for rape being wrong. It is wrong because it fails to function within the relational frame aimed at securing the true humanity of the moral agent and that of the moral patient. Personal perfection requires positive relations with others. The act of rape is wrong precisely because it dehumanises insofar as it undermines the capacity for personal perfection of the victim of rape, as much as it also harms the perpetrator. Positive relations serve as moral enablers for individuals to pursue their perfection. Thus, rape is wrong because it undermines the human capacity for personal perfection that requires positive relations.

The moral insight here is that relationships serve as crucial moral enablers or disablers. The act of rape is a moral disabler insofar as it harms [dehumanises] the woman's capacity to pursue her moral perfection and simultaneously cripples the agent's capacity for personal development. This view of morality is reminiscent of Desmond Tutu's (1999) observation that, in the context of apartheid, the oppressor's humanity was [possibly] as dehumanised as the humanity of the oppressed; hence, the primacy of truth, forgiveness and reconciliation in his account of ubuntu. It is for this reason that the African view puts emphasis on fixing social relationships, because they embody moral possibilities for all (see Ramose 1992). It is also for this reason that African moral thought emphasises that we ought to do as much as possible to reform and re-integrate the offender without neglecting the offended individual in the process, because the moral possibilities and quality of their humanity depends on robust social relationships.

Now, let me turn to a consideration of some concerns and criticisms that may be raised against personhood as a moral theory.

Concerns and criticisms

Below, I will consider two concerns that may be raised about this personhood-based interpretation of ethics. Firstly, this theory of virtue could be criticised for being overly other-regarding in a way that threatens individual uniqueness. If so, it may present the possibility of alienating crucial facets of an individual that are necessary for a robust human life, like autonomy and authenticity (see Tshivhase 2013). The second criticism questions the suitability of perfection as the essence of what morality ought to be about or it doubts that perfection is an appropriate moral ideal for a robust human existence.

I begin by considering the first concern occasioned by the moral view adumbrated in this chapter. There is consensus in the literature that African moral thought tends to lean heavily on the side of other-regarding duties (see Gyekye 1992, 2004; Wiredu 1992, 2009; Metz 2007, 2012b; Ikuenobe 2016; Molefe 2019b, 2019c). This should not come as a surprise given the centrality of the community in African moral thought. In fact, Menkiti (2004, 324) states that 'morality demands a point of view best described as one of beingness-with-others'. Accounting for morality in a way that emphasises sociability raises questions about the individual, her uniqueness and self-regarding duties. In the literature, Tshivhase (2013) eloquently raises this concern regarding the individual, specifically her autonomy and authenticity (which are crucial for accounting for uniqueness). These are possibly undermined by the other-regarding emphasis characteristic of this moral view.

I do not take this to be a serious objection to the perfectionist interpretation of personhood. One reason for this is that a careful analysis of the discourse on personhood reveals that this interpretation does not overlook the self, uniqueness and self-regarding duties. In fact, it is in the first instance a stubbornly self-regarding moral view. The reader will do well to remember the individualism and egoism associated with the discourse on personhood. The idea of individualism points to the fact that the focus of this moral view is on the agent, specifically her character. The goal of morality entirely revolves around the individual and her character. The egoism facet of morality also imposes a duty on the agent to make her own self and her perfection the primary focus. It is these two considerations that I believe best explain why this theory is often accounted for as a *self-realisation* approach to morality, an approach which reveals the centrality of the self (Metz 2007, 330).

In the light of the above, it follows that this theory holds together the self-regarding and other-regarding facets of morality. The goal of morality involves the self-regarding duty of personal perfection, or self-realisation, and the means for achieving this goal requires the agent to relate positively with others. In other words, the emphasis on social relationships is crucial but only for instrumental reasons, since it provides an incubator for individuals to be able to pursue their own moral perfection. Genuine social relationships, therefore, are crucial for individuals to develop virtues associated with personhood and for exploring and unfolding their uniqueness. The importance of social relationships should not surprise us, precisely because virtues associated with personhood are also relational; and even the possibility of exploring one's uniqueness, and hence the best place to develop virtues and uniqueness, is in a social context. David Lutz captures the relationship between the self-regarding and other-regarding facets of personhood in this fashion –

> In a true community, the individual does not pursue the common good instead of his or her own good, *but rather pursues his or her own good through pursuing the common good*. The ethics of a true community does not ask persons to sacrifice their own good in order to promote the good of others, but instead invites them to recognise that they can attain their own true good only by promoting the good of others. (2009, 314; emphasis mine)

The point is well made. The true community is one that affords the individual opportunities to advance her own (self-regarding) good and to promote the good of all (other-regarding duties). This approach to morality refuses to account for the relationships between individuals in conflictual terms. It also refuses to imagine individuals as separate atoms always caught in competition. It imagines autonomy and uniqueness in relational terms, where individual autonomy and uniqueness emerge from being immersed in continuing social relationships — 'I am because we are' (Mbiti 1969; Ikuenobe 2015). Dirk Louw (n.d.) captures this aspect of personhood as follows –

> Thus understood, being a person through other persons translates into '[t]o be human is to affirm one's humanity by recognising the humanity of others in its infinite variety of content and form', or ' human being is a human being through (the otherness of) other human beings.'

I believe this terse response suffices to help the reader appreciate the self-focus of the idea of personhood. I hope it also helps the reader to appreciate the fact that social relationships serve as the means to assist individuals to pursue their own personal perfection. Moreover, as we have just read from Louw, the encounter with the other exposes the infinite difference of the humanity of others, which surely also does not overlook or neglect that of the self. Hence, inasmuch as the idea of personhood embodies a self-regarding ethic through others, it also embodies a communitarian model of uniqueness. It is in the encountering of the other as an embodiment of differences that each individual negotiates her own uniqueness.

The second concern questions the appropriateness or even plausibility of perfection *qua* virtue as a final value that accounts for personhood. This concern could be stated in two related ways. In the first instance, in a way reminiscent of Susan Wolf's (1992) concern about the moral saint, one could argue that the pursuit of personhood (perfection) as the essence of morality would render the life of an agent bland and unappealing. The point here is that there is more to life than the pursuit of moral perfection. The criticism is that the positing and pursuing of personhood as the chief moral goal is bound to make a human life less than robust, since it will miss the many non-moral goods inherent in our cultures, such as sports, recreation and arts. This is the case because the pursuit of moral perfection will consume all the agent's time, resources, and so on.

This concern can be captured in the light of Metz's (2007) criticism of personhood. Metz argues that personhood requires the agent to maximise perfection, which might have unpalatable implications. The requirement to maximise perfection implies that the agent could perform actions that are immoral for the sake of perfection. He gives an example of an individual killing another person for the sake of harvesting their organs to save her own life. The agent could justify the killing of the innocent victim on two grounds. Firstly, she could ground it on the correct supposition that the maximisation of perfection at least requires that the agent avoid death as far as possible. She could take a pill to forget that she killed an individual, which would add to the justification for doing so. Metz suggests that a theory that accommodates the idea that we can kill individuals for the sake of pursuing perfection is surely implausible.

I do believe that there are interpretations of moral perfection as the final good that can satisfactorily address the criticisms raised above. To evade this criticism, it is crucial to distinguish between moral theories that aim at *maximising* a value and those that are moderate insofar as they seek merely to '*satisfice*' it (Byron 2004). The distinction here is between 'choosing what is best and what is satisfactory' (Byron 2004, 1). I believe that the strongest objection to the idea of personhood would be one demonstrating that it is not open to a satisficing interpretation. The satisficing interpretation of the perfection associated with personhood merely requires the agent to pursue satisfactory levels of perfection. One attractive feature of a satisficing moral logic is that 'what is satisfactory is, well, satisfactory. Satisfaction is generally good, and goods of this generality feature prominently in any account of practical reason' (Byron 2004, 1).

I offer two reasons that suggest that the idea of personhood ought to be characterised by the satisficing moral logic. The first reason is that the idea of personhood recognises agent-centred restrictions (or constraints) occasioned by the dignity of individuals (Hurley 1995; McNaughton and Rawling 2006). Wiredu captures the agent-centred restrictions in this fashion –

> Take, for instance, the Akan word for a person, which is *onipa*. A little understanding of Akan will reveal that the word is ambiguous. In contexts of normative comment, the word means a human individual of a certain moral and social standing, as we have explained. On the other hand, in narrative contexts it means simply a human being. Thus, in the normative sense a ten seconds old baby is not yet an *onipa*. But anybody who takes her life in vain has, from an Akan traditional standpoint, trifled with the life of an *onipa*, an embodiment of a speck of the divine substance, and is deserving of the severest sanctions. (2009, 16)

The idea of dignity features above when Wiredu informs us that a ten-seconds-old baby's life cannot be taken away in vain precisely because she has dignity, which he accounts for in terms of her possessing a speck of the divine substance. The simple possession of this property renders the infant a being of superlative value or dignity. In this light, therefore, the point is that in the pursuit of perfection there are restrictions imposed by the dignity of persons. In other words, though personhood requires us to pursue perfection, it cannot be pursued by means that undermine the dignity of individuals. The agent is not required to go to extremes to perfect herself. The requirement is for her to do what she can within the constraints imposed by the dignity of others.

The second reason is embodied in the importance of social relationships in the discourse of personhood. We have already noted that the individual is required to participate in robust social relationships if she is to achieve personhood. Her involvement, however, ought to be a genuine one (Van Niekerk 2013). Two aspects of genuine social relationships are that they must be devoid of selfishness and they must be of the kind that foster cohesion or harmony (Tutu 1999; Shutte 2001). Genuine participation in social relationships requires the agent to relate positively with others, both for their sake and for her own sake. Part of what it means to be in genuine social relationships is that they involve both negative and positive duties towards others. In terms of negative duties, they prohibit us from relating with others in ways that will harm them. We have a duty to refrain from killing them, lying to them and so on even *if* doing such acts would lead to perfection. In positive terms, it loads on us responsibilities to benefit others for their own sake. On my part, it suffices to appreciate the negative duties that are a feature of genuine social relationships to secure the view that the idea of personhood embodies a satisficing moral logic in the pursuit of moral perfection.

Though the idea of personhood is rightly associated with perfection, it embodies what I consider a plausible form of it. The agent is required to pursue satisfactory perfection within constrains imposed by human dignity (her own and that of others) and by social relationships. These objections, (1) that the centrality of other-regarding duties undermines uniqueness and self-regarding duties and (2) that perfection is an inappropriate final value, dissipate because they would carry weight only if personhood requires agents to maximise perfection. All the pursuit of personhood requires is for agents to pursue moral perfection by fostering healthy social relationships, which provide an enabling environment for personal development.

Conclusion

In this chapter, I have offered a philosophical exposition of personhood as a moral theory. I focused on both the theory of virtue and right action, with emphasis on the former. We noted that the idea of personhood posits moral perfection as the goal of morality, which we accounted for in terms of the manifestation of a virtuous character. We also noted some implications of our understanding of moral perfection, namely: the agent-centred nature of morality; moral individualism; moral egoism; and the role of social relationships. We then proceeded to consider personhood as an action-centred theory that accounts for rightness of actions in terms of two features: that the act must lead to the agent realising her moral ideals; and that it must be one that enhances social relationships. We concluded the chapter by considering two objections of the moral theory embodied by personhood.

Notes

1. I advise the reader that this part of the chapter merely provides the highlights of the agent-centred theory of value. It does not fully elaborate or justify some of the claims. Such a full discussion is already present in several of my previous writings (see Molefe 2017a, 2017b, 2018, 2019a, Chapter 3). I provide only the highlights here so as to lay a foundation for the next chapter.

2. I must emphasise that the claim that the fact of being human is necessary for the pursuit of personhood must be construed in a way that is moderate and plausible. Human beings possess the relevant ontological capacity that makes it possible for them to pursue moral perfection. It is not just the fact of being human that does the moral job. There are human beings that do not have the relevant property, and these cannot pursue personhood. We cannot foreclose the possibility of aliens that have the relevant property that allows them to pursue personhood. In my earlier work, I assumed that human nature *qua* human nature, or, some facet of it, is an essential feature of personhood in a way that is objectionable insofar as it entailed speciesism (Molefe 2019a, 51). The reader will see that I offer a weakly anthropocentric view of morality in Chapter 4.

3. I hope the reader will appreciate the necessity of specifying a criterion for right action in a theory that I have explained as agent-centred insofar as it posits the pursuit of moral excellence as the goal of morality. The reason for such a move is to give a complete moral account. To justify this move, consider this comment by Julia Annas –

   > And ancient theories don't just discuss virtue and the good life; they also discuss what is the right thing to do. They can hardly avoid this, since a virtue is a disposition

to do the right thing. In fact a little reflection shows that no sensible theory could be act- or agent-centred in the sense of just considering acts or agents; all theories have to consider both. (1992, 128–129)

The point here is simple; a robust moral theory has to cover both facets, the agent- and act-centred facets. The act-centred facet specifies a path to the former, without which an agent-centred theory becomes empty as the agent is left ignorant regarding what actions lead to moral perfection.

2

Personhood and dignity in African moral-political thought

Introduction

In the previous chapter, we partially examined the robust approach to the ethics of personhood in African philosophy. We considered one side of the moral coin — the moral perfectionism that posits the development of a virtuous character as *the* goal of morality. The aim of this chapter is to articulate a theory of dignity grounded in the idea of personhood. In the previous chapter, we considered the *agent-centred* facet of morality. In this chapter, our focus is on the *patient-centred* facet of the theory of value associated with personhood, specifically how it accounts for moral status or dignity. In the final analysis, I will argue that personhood accounts for dignity in terms of our capacity for virtue [sympathy].

To pursue the view that dignity is a function of our capacity for virtue, I structure this chapter as follows. I begin by clarifying the relationship between the ideas of moral status and dignity. I also stipulate my meta-ethical commitment to ethical naturalism in accounting for dignity. Secondly, I consider two strategies to ground a *conception* of moral status or dignity (the patient-centred theory of value) in the idea of personhood. The first strategy is suggested by Ikuenobe (2017); he construes dignity as a function of the agent's use of her ontological capacities to pursue and achieve personhood. In this view, dignity is a function of moral performance — some kind of moral achievement. I offer two reasons why we should not take this approach to theorising about dignity in the light of personhood seriously. The second strategy — gleaned from Menkiti (1984) and Gyekye (1992) — grounds dignity in a particular ontological capacity of human nature, specifically the capacity for virtue, where I propose that sympathy is a central virtue in the discourse of personhood.

I argue that this second view offers a more robust personhood-based theory of dignity insofar as it captures the egalitarianism associated with the discourse on dignity in modern moral-political theory. I then continue, by way of conclusion, to elaborate on an African conception of dignity *qua* the capacity for sympathy by reflecting on the words used to refer to sympathy in African languages.

Let me begin by making two clarificatory comments. Firstly, I would like to clarify the relationship between moral status and dignity. Thereafter, I will examine the idea of dignity in African languages.

The relationship between moral status and dignity

The idea of moral status involves identifying beings of moral significance — those that count as moral patients. Moral agents owe such beings direct moral duties of respect, or duties based on the rights of those entities. Scholars tend to consider the idea of moral status to be one that admits of degrees, which means that some beings might have more of it, some less and others none. (DeGrazia 2008, 2013; Toscano 2011; Behrens 2011). At least, I take this view of it in the book. One reason some scholars suggest that we take this idea to admit of degrees is the fact that it best explains how we can resolve trade-off cases. Take, for example, a situation in which one must either drive over a normal adult human being or a cat; most people would be more morally comfortable driving over the cat. The reason for this is simply the fact that a human being is considered to have greater moral status than a cat (see Metz 2012b). In this light, it makes sense to draw a distinction between beings who have partial moral status and those with great moral status (see Metz 2012b). The idea of dignity is taken to be tantamount to the idea of possessing greater moral status. In fact, more accurately, scholars construe dignity in terms of *full moral status* (Toscano 2011). The following comment by Waldron regarding the concept of dignity as the possession of full moral status should, therefore, not be surprising –

> The distinctive contribution that 'dignity' makes to human rights discourse is associated, paradoxically, with the idea of rank: once associated with hierarchical differentiations of rank and status, 'dignity' now conveys the idea that all human persons belong to the same rank and *that rank is very high indeed*. (2012, 201; emphasis mine)

The idea of dignity, historically, is associated with rank and status — *dignitas* — which 'represented the honour and respectful treatment attributed to someone on the basis of their high social status, in particular noblemen and men in high offices' (Michael 2014, 13). *Dignitas* as a high status was the reserve of a select few. The strategy of thinking of dignity in terms of moral status amounts to the view that all human beings are special and deserve special moral recognition because of their status *qua* human beings. Rosen (2012) captures this strategy in terms of what he calls the 'expanding circle' narrative. He comments on it in this fashion –

> From this perspective, the quality of dignity, once a property of a social elite, has, like the idea of rights, *been extended outward and downward until it has come to apply to all human beings*. This is all part of the great, long process by which the fundamental equality of human being has come to be accepted. (2012, 8; emphasis mine)

The essence of this quotation is to echo the view that the idea of dignity refers to a property now equally possessed by all human beings. In other words, the high rank of dignity now includes even the lowest of all human beings. Hence, to claim that human beings have dignity is to specify the high rank of their (moral) status.

Dignity in these terms is generally construed to be characterised by three features. The first involves the *stringent constraints* not to interfere, harm, undermine or instrumentalise a being of high value (McNaughton and Rawling 2006; Donnelly 2009; Jaworska and Tannenbaum 2018). The agent-centred restrictions (constraints) associated with beings of dignity are stringent insofar as they signal that there are almost no exceptions to their inviolability (Hurley 1995; Toscano 2011; Rosen 2012).

The second feature concerns the fact that we have *strong duties* to aid a being of dignity (Jaworska and Tannenbaum 2018). If we encounter a being of dignity in a situation where she requires our assistance and we can help without a great inconvenience on our part, we would have failed to conduct ourselves appropriately if we do not assist. Beings of dignity attract general duties that moral agents, all things being equal, ought to exercise towards them (Loschke 2017).

The last feature is captured in terms of the idea of equality or the 'equal wrongness thesis' (Jaworska and Tannenbaum 2018). The thesis captures the egalitarianism associated with beings of dignity. That is, all things being equal, if a particular act is wrong when performed towards a being of dignity, it must be equally wrong if performed towards another being of dignity. Dignity plays an important role in equalising moral patients. This last facet captures the egalitarianism inherent in the idea of dignity.

The idea of dignity in African languages

Now that I have clarified how I understand the relationship between moral status and dignity, I proceed to consider one way to ground dignity on the idea of personhood in the tradition of African philosophy. I begin below by commenting on African words used to capture the idea of dignity.

Chapter 2

The reader would have noticed that my engagement with the idea of dignity thus far relies on the English literature in philosophy and related fields. I have not employed local African languages to consider its meaning and philosophical implications. I suggest that scholars who attempt to reflect on dignity in African philosophy do not usually consider local languages and their philosophical implications (see Gyekye 1992; Wiredu 1996a; Ilesanmi 2001; Deng 2004; Metz 2012; Ikuenobe 2017, 2018; Makwinja 2019). For my part, I do not focus on local languages because I take the idea of personhood to embody a *universal* concept, which is expressed differently in different languages and cultures. Moreover, I avoid invoking local words for dignity because they tend to imply a religious metaphysics; and I have stipulated a secular meta-ethical approach in this book.[1]

Consider the following evidence for the idea that the meaning of dignity in African languages embodies a spiritual metaphysics. In IsiZulu, Ndebele, and Swati, for example — spoken largely in South Africa, Zimbabwe and Swaziland, respectively — the word for dignity is *isithunzi*. The idea of dignity is related to -*thunzi*, literally, a shadow. In other words, just as a tree has a shadow (*um-thunzi*), a human being has *isithunzi*. The same semantic logic is true of isiXhosa where dignity is translated as *isidima*, and in seSotho, where it is *serithi*. In seSotho, shadow is translated as *murithi*, and, as such, a tree has *murithi*. A human being, on the other hand, has *serithi*. The metaphysics lurking in the background of talking of dignity in terms of the imagery of a shadow is that of the idea of vitality (Tempels 1959). Dignity, in this view, is a function of possessing vitality, which is usually understood as a spiritual energy that emanates from God (Bikopo and Van Borgaert 2009, 44).

I distance myself from the view of dignity associated with such local languages, particularly among the Nguni and Sotho languages. I believe it is not plausible. I think the vitalist approach muddies the waters since it implies its own ethical system of morality and dignity — a vitality- or life-based ethics (see Tempels 1959; Shutte 2001; Imafidon 2013). I do not find approaches accounting for dignity and personhood in terms of vitality or life to be compelling because they never quite explain why we must base a moral system on such thick and controversial metaphysical systems. It is also important to notice that scholars of African thought require us to accept this metaphysical view on the basis of anthropological evidence, and not on any sound philosophical justification of ethical supernaturalism. Moreover, I tend to agree with those who believe that accounting for dignity in terms of life or vitality produces a parochial moral system best geared to dealing with issues of life and death. Morality has to do with much more than life and death (see Metz 2012c). In any event, for my part, I stipulate a secular interpretation of personhood and dignity. I also believe that this secular view, which manifests in the works of pioneers of personhood like Menkiti and Gyekye, entails a robust conception of dignity. It is this secular view of dignity associated with personhood that I hope to unfold in this discussion. Below, I consider Ikuenobe's view of dignity.

Ikuenobe's personhood-based view of dignity

Above, we characterised the concept of dignity as one that identifies beings of high value in the natural domain. Below, we proceed to consider grounds that grant some entity moral status or dignity. In what follows, I will consider (what I take to be) one unsuccessful attempt to ground dignity on the idea of personhood. Recently, Ikuenobe (2017) in the article *The Communal Basis for Moral Dignity: An African Perspective* defends a novel account of dignity (see also Ikuenobe 2018).[2] He believes that the idea of personhood salient among African moral cultures promises a plausible conception of dignity. Ikuenobe's project is two-fold. On the one hand, he rejects those conceptions of dignity that account for it entirely in terms of some ontological property. On the other, he seeks to ground dignity in some kind of moral achievement *qua* personhood.

In the literature — both from the Western and African perspectives — dignity is typically understood as a function of possessing a particular ontological feature, be it rationality, a basic capability, the divine image, *okra*, or a capacity for relationships (Gyekye 1992; Kant [1785] 1996; Wiredu 1996a; Nussbaum 2011; Metz 2011). I might add that this is the dominant view in the literature regarding how to conceptualise the idea of dignity. It occurs to me that Ikuenobe is not satisfied with this approach to dignity because it seems to be committing the naturalistic fallacy. It seems that his major dispute against this way of conceptualising value is that it is not entirely clear how some beings can be considered intrinsically valuable merely because they possess a particular ontological feature. That is, how can we derive unconditional respect for human beings simply from the fact that they possess certain ontological features?

According to Ikuenobe, a correct view must insist that ontological capacities in themselves are only instrumentally valuable. That is, ontological properties are necessary but not sufficient for dignity. Dignity, according to Ikuenobe, is a function of 'the capacity for, and manifestation of, self-respect and respect for, and responsibility to, others' (2017, 438). In other words, dignity is realised when the agent lives up to the standards of excellence that are consistent with her ontological features, specifically by achieving personhood. Ikuenobe summarises his view of dignity in this fashion –

> My view indicates that dignity is grounded in the idea of moral personhood as *one who uses one's capacity properly* to promote harmonious communal living. (2017, 438; emphasis mine)

The central facet of the idea of personhood is the idea of moral conduct or performance oriented towards and exuding excellence. Ikuenobe construes the idea of dignity in terms of the quality of the agent's moral conduct insofar as it is consistent with the norms of moral excellence that promote certain social goods. The essential facet of this way of construing dignity abandons the dominant view, which construes it as a function of merely possessing some capacity of human nature such as rationality (Rosen 2012; Michael 2014; Miller 2017). Instead, it prefers to construe dignity in terms of moral achievement, related directly to how one uses the relevant property. In this view, dignity is possible because we have certain ontological capacities, but it is the proper use of these capacities that results in its emergence. Dignity is not a given.

Objections against Ikuenobe's view of dignity

I raise two objections against this way of employing the idea of personhood to account for dignity in terms of moral achievement, which is best captured in terms of a virtuous character *qua* personhood. Firstly, the hallmark of the modern idea of dignity is its commitment to egalitarianism. The idea of egalitarianism is commonly defined as referring to 'all theories that favor according people equal…degrees or amounts of something, even where that something is a non-material good like concern or moral authority' (Carter 2011, 540). The essence of egalitarian theories is essentially defined by their espousal of the value of *equality* (Dworkin 1981a, 1981b; Pojman 1995). This approach to moral-political theory — grounded in the primacy of the value of equality — is usually referred to as the 'abstract egalitarian plateau' (Dowrkin, 1980a, 1981b). In this moral-political view, social justice is a function of 'treating people equally' (Kymlicka 1990, 7).

The advantage of accounting for dignity strictly in terms of some ontological property is that it captures the egalitarianism characteristic of plausible moral and political theorisation defined by the idea of treating persons (human beings) as equals (Kymlicka 1990, 7). The egalitarianism characteristic of the idea of dignity is captured thus by Brennan and Lo –

> The modern notion of dignity drops the hierarchical elements implicit in the meaning of *dignitas*, and uses the term so that all human beings must have equal dignity, regardless of their virtues, merits, social and political status, or any other contingent features. (2007, 47)

This approach to moral-political theorisation about dignity secures the equality of all human beings by grounding it in the mere possession of some ontological feature. In other words, human beings have dignity merely because they are the kind of beings that they are, without regard to performance at all. This egalitarian feature of dignity is also captured thus by Glenn Hughes –

> The drafters [of the Universal Declaration of Human Rights] solved this problem by indicating that human beings have rights because of their intrinsic dignity — because human beings, *due to qualities they possess*, have a special value or distinctive worth that in each case and without exception should be respected and nourished. (2011, 3; emphasis mine)

In other words, human beings are equal and deserve equal moral regard, usually captured in terms of human rights, because they possess certain ontological features, and no more. The theoretical and practical advantage of grounding dignity strictly and solely on some qualities human beings possess is simply the fact that it equalises them and demands that we treat them with equal concern and respect.

The problem with Ikuenobe's view of dignity, in my view, is that it repudiates the ontological approach to dignity in favour of a performance-based one. This sacrifices the attractive feature of egalitarianism without indicating what the moral-political advantage of an achievement-oriented approach would be. The moment dignity is a function of moral performance and excellence, it means that we will be creating an inegalitarian society where, for example, moral and political goods will be a function of moral performance. Those individuals that do well will get access to more moral and political goods, and those that fail will gain less, if anything at all.

The idea of universal suffrage becomes applicable as a potent example of how objectionable the view of dignity under consideration is. Each citizen is entitled to equal political participation and opportunities in society merely because they are human. In Ikuenobe's view, it is not entirely clear how we will deal with the issue of universal suffrage, particularly if moral excellence is the basis for dignity. The implication is that those with dignity, those who have achieved personhood, will either vote more or their vote will count more, and villains' votes will count less, if at all. I raise this case of universal suffrage to point out the fact that this idea of personhood is intrinsically inegalitarian because it bases respect on moral performance in which individuals could never be equal. Those that perform worse will deserve less respect, with some deserving none for their appalling conduct. This can never be a suitable basis for a fair moral and political system, particularly in the international legal culture of rights which has engulfed our world.

I insist that a plausible understanding of dignity construes it as the kind of property 'that none of us has by merit, that none of us can receive from others, and that no one can take from us' (Pannenberg 1991, 177). In Ikuenobe's view, conversely, we have dignity by merit, we receive it from others, and they can even take it from us, depending on our moral performance. The major weakness of Ikuenobe's view is that it loses the egalitarianism associated with dignity and it fails to secure the culture of rights grounded in it, and the theoretical and practical advantage of his proposed view of dignity is not made overt.

Secondly, I reject this idea of dignity because it fails to accommodate the young (in this instance, I have infants in mind) in the moral community. This is the case precisely because Ikuenobe's (2017, 461; emphasis mine) conception of dignity insists that 'human capacities are only an *instrumental good*; they are only a means for a good life…' The upshot of this view is that the possession of a capacity is insufficient for the possession of dignity. Dignity, in this view, requires the actual use of one's ontological features to achieve personhood. Since infants are in no position to exercise their human capacities, it should follow that they have no moral status and no dignity.

A possible defence aimed at including infants in the moral community might involve invoking the fact that they have the *potential* to use such property in the future. This move does not quite solve the problem though, because, remember, mere possession of a property is instrumentally good, but it is the actual use that 'creates' dignity. So, the possession of a potential to use this property cannot secure dignity. Dignity arises *only* in contexts of (positive) use.

To respond to this objection, Ikuenobe makes the following argument –

> The idea of respecting unconditionally those who are not capable of acting to earn respect is supported by the moral principle of 'ought implies can', which indicates that you cannot hold people responsible for what is impossible for them. (2017, 464)

It is urgent that we consider whether the principle of 'ought implies can' is sufficient to secure the view that we owe unconditional respect to those (like infants) who are not capable of earning it. I remain unconvinced that this principle can do this. It is true that we cannot hold an individual responsible for what they cannot do. But accepting this fact, in and of itself, leaves us with a theoretical gap — the question still remains what the ground for unconditional respect to the young could be. If dignity is a function entirely of the actual use of the relevant capacity, the following is necessarily true. Firstly, the possession of the relevant ontological property is necessary but not sufficient for the possession of dignity. The sufficient condition stipulated in Ikuenobe's view of dignity is the actual use of the property. Secondly, the principle of 'ought implies can' instructs us not to expect the young to have dignity just yet, but it does, as Ikuenobe's suggests, secure unconditional respect for the young. In this light, the question we should be asking is not whether we can hold the young to be responsible or not; here we agree on the basis of 'ought implies can' principle. The question that remains, however, is — on what ground do we owe the young unconditional respect?[3]

To clarify my case, if being a champion is a function only of running and winning in a competition, then I ought to run and win to be granted the status of a 'champion'.

In the event that I have an accident that makes it impossible for me to run, it does not follow that I should be unconditionally granted the status of being a champion on the basis of 'ought implies can'. At best, my fans may feel great pity for me and wish me a speedy recovery. In terms of the rules of the game, I am not owed any kind of respect — let alone unconditional respect — given that I am not in a position to fulfil the specified conditions for winning.

Contrary to this performance-based view of dignity, however, is the capacity-based view, which I believe *can* secure the unconditional respect that we owe to the young. In this view, the young are owed unconditional respect merely because they possess the relevant potential. In what follows, I articulate what I take to be a more plausible interpretation of a personhood-based view of dignity — a capacity-based conception of dignity *qua* personhood based on Menkiti's and Gyekye's adumbrations.

Personhood and dignity in African philosophy

In what follows, I propose to construct an under-explored alternative theory of dignity grounded in the idea of personhood, which is inspired by Menkiti and Gyekye. In keeping with what I take to be standard and plausible approaches to theorising about dignity, I will base it on some ontological feature. I wish to make it clear that the idea of dignity that I will be considering here is already implicitly present in Menkiti's exposition of the agent-centred notion of personhood; and, it is somewhat explicit in Gyekye's adumbrations on the same topic.

Below, I begin by revisiting Menkiti's thoughts on personhood with the aim of distilling a conception of moral status/dignity embodied in his philosophical elucidations.

Menkiti on moral status (dignity)

I remind the reader that in my own philosophical exposition of Menkiti's analysis of personhood, I identify at least three distinct concepts of personhood (Molefe 2016; Molefe 2019a, 2019b; see also Metz 2013a, 13). I believe that Menkiti's first concept of personhood is the idea of personhood *qua* personal identity. He defines this idea of personhood in terms of the 'environing community' (Menkiti 1984, 170). By 'environing community' Menkiti has in mind socio-cultural facts and resources necessary for socialising or humanising a human being. Menkiti associates *this* idea of personhood with an 'individual [who] comes to see himself as a man'; develops certain cognitive and conative features (or what Menkiti refers to as the 'constitution of his mental disposition and attitudes'); acquires a particular 'language'; and finally reduces this idea of a person to the statement that the 'self-identity which the individual comes to possess cannot be made sense of except by

Chapter 2

reference to these collective facts' (1984, 172). Metz commenting on this idea of personhood captures it in this fashion –

> It is worth noting a third, descriptive understanding of personhood, one that is arguably shared by both traditions. This third sense of the word 'person' is roughly the idea of an individual aware of itself over time and able to act consequent to deliberation, such that human babies are not yet persons and God is always already a person (on some conceptions). This concept of personhood is ontological, and does not include any moral ideas about values or norms. (2013a, 12–13)

One crucial insight to note from Metz's analysis is that this concept of personhood *qua* personal identity is ontological. It is ontological insofar as it specifies some descriptive features — cultural facts — as the basis for according personhood to individuals.

The second concept of personhood present in Menkiti's exposition is a moral one: it is what I have been referring to as the agent-centred notion of personhood. Menkiti (1984, 171) conceives of this idea as processual, and he construes this process as one that involves a transformation from merely being human to being an entity characterised by moral excellence (see Eze 2018). The moral excellence that defines personhood is consequent to the agent having developed 'a widened ethical maturity', which explains why the agent will be characteristically 'generous…hospitable… friendly, and caring and compassionate' or what Gyekye refers to as embodying the 'moral practice' of other-regarding virtues (Menkiti 1984, 176; Gyekye 1992, 109; Tutu 1999, 35). It is this idea of personhood *qua* 'human excellence or virtue', Metz (2013a, 12–13) informs us, that is salient 'in [the] sub-Saharan context' (see also Wiredu 1992, 2004, 2009; Molefe 2019a, 2019b).

The third notion of personhood present in Menkiti's work appears in two different ways. In the first instance, Menkiti believes that his notion of personhood (the agent-centred notion) is similar, or very close, to the one expressed in John Rawls moral-political philosophy. Menkiti reports this association between his and Rawls' view of personhood in this manner –

> John Rawls, of the Western-born philosophers, comes closest to a recognition of this importance of ethical sense in the definition of personhood. In *A Theory of Justice* he makes explicit part of what is meant by the general ethical requirement of respect for persons, noting that those who are capable of a sense of justice are owed the duties of justice, with this capability construed in its sense of a potentiality which may or may not have been realised. (1984, 177)

It is crucial to notice that Menkiti believes that Rawls comes close to recognising the ethical sense in the definition of personhood. I think that Menkiti rightly

identifies that Rawls has a moral concept of 'personhood' in mind, but he is wrong to say that it comes close to his own. Note that Menkiti's description of Rawls's idea of personhood indicates that it is a patient-centred rather than an agent-centred one. He talks of this idea in terms of the ethical requirement of respect for persons.

At this stage, we may be confused because the phrase 'respect for persons' is ambiguous regarding which notion of respect is involved: is it *recognition* or *appraisal* respect? (Darwall 1977). Recognition respect tracks and responds to ontology. Appraisal respect tracks and responds to (moral) excellence. Menkiti solves this ambiguity for us by noting that the respect imagined here is one that is owed to entities that are *capable of a sense of justice* — this I read as a reference to a particular ontological capacity. It is crucial to notice that this idea allocates respect merely because the entity in question has a particular ontological property, without regard to its use. Menkiti notes that the respect imagined here has nothing to do with whether this capability is realised or not. In other words, it is not the use of this capability for justice that matters for respect; to be included in the moral-political community, it is sufficient just to be an entity that has this capacity.

The idea of personhood that Menkiti associates with Rawls is what we have been referring to as the patient-centred notion of personhood, which is tantamount to the idea of moral status or dignity. Another crucial piece of evidence that the idea under consideration is that of moral status or dignity is the fact that Menkiti associates it with the idea of justice. One of the central features of the discourse of justice is *treating people as equals*, as we noted above (Kymlicka 1990). It is because the idea of dignity is equalising that it is useful as a means of capturing the ideal of social justice (see Metz 2013a; Behrens 2013; Molefe 2018). It is not clear in the text that Menkiti was aware that the notion of personhood discussed by Rawls is distinct from the one he was considering (i.e. that it was patient-centred rather than agent-centred).

This idea of personhood *qua* moral status/dignity occurs again in Menkiti's analysis in the context where he is considering the tendency to extend the moral language of rights or justice to animals. Menkiti (1984, 177) describes philosophical moves that extend moral language and duties of justice to animals as 'dangerous tendencies fashionable in some philosophical circles…' He (1984, 177) rejects this move because it is 'bound to undermine, sooner or later, the clearness of our conception of what it means to be a person'. He also warns us of this

> …peculiar philosophy in which the constitutive elements in the definition of human personhood have become blurred through unwarranted extensions to non-human entities. (1984, 177)

Here, Menkiti repudiates the extension of the moral language to animals because it undermines what he calls 'our clear conception of personhood' or deviates from a proper understanding of the 'constitutive elements of human personhood' (1984, 177).

The insight that seems to emerge from Menkiti's adumbrations is that there is an ontological difference between human beings and animals that makes all the moral difference regarding the extension or denial of rights. In other words, human beings possess particular ontological properties that make them beings towards which we can properly extend rights, or beings towards which we have duties of justice. The same is not the case regarding animals, since they lack these constitutive elements of personhood.

The reader may here press me to clarify how ontology may lead to moral differences between human beings and animals. The simple answer is — we need merely recognise and appreciate the very nature of the idea of moral status/dignity, or the idea of recognition respect (Darwall 1977). This idea requires us to respect those kinds of entities that have morally relevant ontological properties. If it is true, as Menkiti appears to believe, that human beings, and not animals, have the relevant ontological features, then it is correct to ascribe rights to them. Then in the light of this exposition of Menkiti's discussion of personhood *qua* moral status, it becomes urgent for us to specify the ontological property that grounds moral status or dignity on the part of human beings, and not animals. Menkiti captures this view of dignity as follows –

> If it is generally conceded, then, that persons are the sort of entities that are owed the duties of justice, it must also be allowed that each time we find an ascription of any of the various rights implied by these duties of justice, the conclusion naturally follows that the possessor of the rights in question cannot be other than a person. That is so because the basis of such rights ascription has now been made dependent on a possession of *a capacity for moral sense*, a capacity, which though it need not be realised, is nonetheless made most evident by a concrete exercise of duties of justice towards others in the ongoing relationships of everyday life. (1984, 177; emphasis mine)

In this line of reasoning, Menkiti grounds moral status or dignity on the human capacity for moral sense. In other words, in the light of Menkiti's adumbrations on the agent-centred notion of personhood, it follows that he accounts for dignity in terms of the capacity to pursue or achieve moral personhood. In Menkiti's view, moral sense is necessary for a being to be able to live a life of moral excellence; it is the capacity to pursue such a life that attracts rights ascriptions to human beings and not to animals. It is important to note the line by Menkiti that this capacity need not be realised. It is, in and of itself, sufficient to secure moral status.

I think the above considerations undoubtedly point to a personhood-based conception of moral status. I hope not to be construed here to mean that this is the view of dignity that Menkiti himself subscribes to; it is one that I believe, however, can be read off his work and is most consistent with his commitment to account for morality in terms of virtue (personhood). Below, I proceed to demonstrate that Gyekye's philosophical explication of personhood embodies the same view of dignity *qua* the capacity for moral sense.

Gyekye, personhood and moral status (dignity)

In my view, Gyekye supports the interpretation of dignity *qua* moral sense or the capacity to pursue virtue espoused by Menkiti above. It is crucial to notice that the passage I am about to consider emerges in the context of Gyekye responding to Menkiti's adumbrations on personhood. Gyekye endorses the idea of personhood *qua* virtue as a central article of African moral cultures (see Gyekye 1992, 1997, 2010). In one place, he comments thus regarding personhood — 'the judgment, "he is a person", means "he has a good character", "he is generous", "he is peaceful", "he is humble", "he has respect for others"'. This is a comment about the agent-centred notion of personhood. We might want to philosophically explore whether Gyekye connects the agent-centred notion of personhood with a specific view of dignity. I think he does, though this part of his work has not received enough attention in the literature.

To begin, it is important to recognise that Gyekye offers three distinct conceptions of dignity in his 1992 essay. The first account of dignity grounds it in the possession of a divine property — *okra* — or appeals to the status of being a child of God (1992, 110, 114). In other words, merely because a human being has this divine feature, we owe her equal and unconditional moral regard. The second conception grounds dignity in the autonomous dimensions of human nature (1992, 111–113). Gyekye (1997, 67) goes as far as to state that the human property of autonomy is intrinsically valuable. The first view of dignity is religious insofar as it invokes a divine property to ground it. The second view of dignity is secular insofar as it invokes a natural human property of autonomy.

It is interesting to notice that these two conceptions of dignity are not directly connected to the idea of personhood that is at issue between Menkiti and Gyekye, or, more precisely, that Gyekye does not draw out any relationship between *okra* and *autonomy* as conceptions of dignity and the idea of personhood. It is equally notable that Gyekye is committed to the view that the idea of dignity is a central feature of the Afro-communitarian moral-political order, but that he remains indifferent with regards to assessing which of the views of dignity occurring in his essay is most African and plausible as a ground for an authentic Afro-communitarian moral-political view.

The last conception of dignity that emerges from Gyekye's moral theory is more interesting and relevant to this book. It is directly connected to the agent-centred notion of personhood crucial to Afro-communitarianism. Here is Gyekye's view of dignity –

> The foregoing discussion of some morally significant expressions in the Akan language or judgements made about the conduct of persons suggests a conception of moral personhood; *a person is defined in terms of moral qualities or capacities*: a human person is a being who has a moral sense and is capable of making moral judgements. (1992, 110; emphasis mine)

Gyekye here makes the direct link between the agent-centred notion of personhood — what he refers to as the Akan language or judgments made about the conduct of persons — and the patient-centred notion of personhood — what he talks of as the moral conception of personhood. Note that Gyekye expressly states that the agent-centred notion characterised by moral conduct suggests a moral conception of personhood. We should note that here we are dealing with two moral concepts of personhood, where one is said to suggest the other. We should appreciate this as evidence that what he refers to as 'a moral conception of personhood' is the idea of moral status or dignity. The evidence is secured by how he defines 'a moral conception of personhood' in terms of moral qualities or capacities, which I take to refer to some ontological property of human nature. Gyekye informs us that human beings have ontological features of moral agency (what he calls moral sense) and that he understands human beings in terms of their capability to make moral judgments. The crucial insight here is that the agent-centred idea of personhood is possible because human beings have the capacity for moral sense.

Just before saying this, Gyekye (1992, 109) is even more specific regarding the relationship between the agent-centred and patient-centred notions of personhood. He is very particular about the nature of the capacity that grounds dignity *qua* the idea of personhood. Gyekye begins by informing us that 'the pursuit or practice of moral virtue is held as intrinsic to the conception of a person' (1992, 109). What does he mean by stating that the practice of virtue is *intrinsic* to the conception of personhood? One interesting way to understand Gyekye is in terms of the underlying idea of dignity that informs the discourse of personhood (virtue). Note that he informs us that 'there are moral virtues that the human person is *capable* of displaying in his conduct. And because he is thought to be *capable* of displaying those virtues, it is *expected* that he would…' (1992, 109). Therefore, when Gyekye states that the practice of virtue is intrinsic to the conception of personhood, he is bringing to the fore the metaphysical view underpinning the agent-centred view of personhood.

A human being is believed to come into the world wired in a particular way. It is this wiring that makes a human being capable of pursuing and achieving personhood. It is this belief that human beings are wired with the capacity to pursue personhood that informs the expectation that they ought to display moral virtue. Gyekye is specific about the nature of the capacity that accounts for dignity in this fashion –

> It means, further, that the human person is considered to possess *an innate capacity for virtue*, for performing morally right actions and therefore should be treated as a morally responsible agent. (1992, 109; emphasis mine)

In this light, we can rightly conclude that the idea of personhood embodies a particular conception of dignity; human beings have moral status/dignity insofar as they have the capacity for virtue. Human beings ought to be respected and treated with the utmost moral regard because they have the ability to pursue human excellence. It is this moral sense that merits respect.

It is important to emphasise that to possess the innate capacity for moral virtue is not the same as to imply or even suggest that the pursuit of moral excellence is easy, guaranteed or automatic. It simply registers three crucial philosophical considerations. Firstly, it informs us about the metaphysics that grounds the discourse of personhood. It highlights the fact that morality is possible precisely because human beings have the capacity for virtue. Secondly, it explains the expectation that human beings ought to achieve personhood, and therefore lead virtuous lives (see Wingo 2006; Gyekye 2010). Finally, it explains why African scholars tend to hold a positive view of human nature, one in which humans are expected to excel rather than be drowned by original sin.

In the light of Menkiti's and Gyekye's adumbrations above, it follows that they account for human dignity in terms of the human capacity for virtue. In this view, it is not the actual acquisition or display of virtue that grants dignity; rather one has it because one has the relevant ontological feature. At this stage, it might help our understanding of African moral thought if we can be precise regarding what we mean when we account for dignity in terms of the 'capacity for *virtue*'. Is there a distinctive psycho-moral mechanism that explains this capacity for virtue in the discourse of personhood? Below, I attempt to be more precise regarding this conception of dignity *qua* the capacity for virtue.

Personhood, dignity and sympathy

I believe there is a distinctive psycho-moral mechanism inherent in the discourse of personhood *qua* dignity, but it has not yet been philosophically unfolded. Remember that scholars of African thought cite various virtues as characteristic or even constitutive of personhood, be they generosity, love, friendliness or kindness, and so on. (Gyekye 1992; Mokgoro 1998; Tutu 1999). Is there a central virtue that we can invoke to account for all of the others, such that to have personhood simply is to have this virtue in the first place? I believe that such a unity of virtues is possible in the light of the discourse of personhood. The first clue we have in searching for such a unifying feature of these disparate virtues is that they are relational in nature — they are essentially other-regarding.

I think Kwasi Wiredu's (1992, 1996) exposition of his moral theory of sympathetic impartiality is helpful as a way of being more precise about the virtue that holds these together. In the exposition of his moral philosophy, Wiredu suggests that the central virtue that encapsulates and can be construed to be generative of all other virtues involved in personhood is that of sympathy. Wiredu (1996, 71) informs us that sympathy is 'the root of all moral virtue'. To press the concept of sympathy-as-the-*root*-of-all-virtues to its moral limit may amount to the view that it is in some sense foundational in all discourse of personhood *qua* moral perfection (virtue). The foundational status of sympathy could be interpreted to mean that all other virtues are dependent on and expressive of it. This is why Wiredu states that it is 'the root of *all* moral virtue'. Alternatively, we could characterise the relationship as one in which sympathy is the root while the other virtues are its fruits. Or, that sympathy is *generative* of all other virtues, such as kindness, compassion, generosity, love and so on. Giving sympathy this foundational status means that to possess personhood is simply to be sympathetic; and *the* goal of morality is to develop this moral capacity.

In the light of the above exposition, we can more precisely account for the personhood-based view of dignity in terms of the capacity for sympathy. In this light, what is distinctive about human nature, when it comes to intrinsic moral qualities, is our capacity for sympathy. Therefore, the moral sense (capacity) that Menkiti and Gyekye take to be definitive of dignity is that of sympathy.

It is important to notice that Wiredu does not go on to give us a sense of how he understands the idea of sympathy in African moral thought. The idea of sympathy features significantly among those scholars that take a sentimentalist view of morality (see Slote 2010). I think the idea of sympathy in African languages could teach us a great deal about how to think about morality *qua* personhood, if personhood can ultimately be reduced to sympathy the way I am suggesting here. In considering this, I will limit myself to two languages that I am most familiar with: isiZulu and seSotho.

In isiZulu, the word 'sympathy' can be literally translated as *u-zwelo*. In seSotho, it is *kutlwelo-bohloko*. It is my view that these words are strictly equivalent in terms of meaning. The root of these words is –*zwa* (Zulu) and *tlwa* (Sotho). These words (infinitive verbs) literally mean 'to hear'. In this light, the idea of sympathy is based on an analogy with hearing, which suggests that the word 'sympathy' (in the light of these African languages) refers to the ability to feel for ('hear') another. In other words, just as we can hear sound from others when they speak; so, in the moral sphere, we should be able to 'hear' others' moral plight. The idea of sympathy thus refers to the human ability or capacity to be sensitive and responsive to (to 'hear') the condition of others. In the discourse of personhood, it is this capacity for sympathy *qua* the moral ability, figuratively conceptualised through hearing, which is the hallmark of a virtuous individual. Hence, the high regard placed on other-regarding virtues like care, compassion, forgiveness, sharing, friendliness and so on since they are expressive of the underlying moral emotion of sympathy.

Conclusion

In this chapter, we considered the other side of the moral coin related to the concept of personhood. On the one side, in the previous chapter, we considered personhood as a theory of virtue — where it construes morality as a practice of the agent pursuing moral perfection. Moral perfection is understood almost exclusively in terms of other-regarding virtues (duties) like compassion, generosity, love, friendliness and so on. On the other side, the focus is on the theory of moral status/dignity embodied by personhood. We began by rejecting a performance-based view of dignity defended by Ikuenobe. We rejected this view largely because it abandons the egalitarianism that makes the modern idea of dignity compelling and plausible. It also fails to secure the moral status of young children — those who have not yet reached the age of reason. We then continued by considering a view of dignity that can be drawn from Menkiti's and Gyekye's adumbrations on personhood. In this view, dignity is accounted for in terms of the capacity for virtue. We observed that this *capacity for virtue* can be more precisely reduced to the capacity for *sympathy*. I think this view of dignity should be taken seriously for several reasons.

Firstly, to base dignity on the human capacity for sympathy secures the egalitarianism crucial to grounding a robust polity. It allows for the invocation, for example, of the franchise of rights. Secondly, this idea of dignity is promising since it eschews the weaknesses associated with the Ikuenobe's conception of dignity *qua* personhood. It seems to have the theoretical resources available to secure the moral status of the young (infants) by invoking the property of potential (see Gyekye 1992, 114). It also promises to offer a useful opportunity for comparison with recent understandings of dignity in care ethics, which grounds it in the capacity for care (see Gilligan 2013; Miller 2017).

Another crucial distinction that will help our appreciation of the discourse of dignity is to keep the difference between having dignity (as a matter of fact) and living a decent or dignified life (as a matter of moral performance) in mind. To have dignity is simply to specify the fact that an entity has such and such ontological properties that render it intrinsically and superlatively valuable. This fact of having dignity requires the recognition of certain ontological features, in our case, the capacity for sympathy — this is what is sometimes referred to as 'status dignity' (Miller 2017, 112). Living a decent or dignified life is also a function, in part, of the agent living up to the possibilities of their ontological equipment — this is what is sometimes called 'performative dignity' (Miller 2017, 112).[4] In other words, in the view of personhood articulated here, if the possession of the capacity for virtue (as sympathy) is what makes human beings possessors of status dignity, then a decent life (a performatively dignified one) is a function of living a sympathetic life. Failure on the part of the agent to live a virtuous life is not tantamount to a loss of (status) dignity; it is a failure to live a truly human life (a failure in performative dignity). Hence, we do not *achieve* (status) dignity; it is a (performatively) *dignified life* that we achieve or fail to achieve. Hence, to achieve personhood is tantamount to living a decent human life, and not the achievement of (status) dignity itself. It is this distinction that is threatened by Ikuenobe, and which prompted my criticism of his view. It is a step in the wrong direction to reduce all dignity to performative dignity, as he does.

In Chapter 1, we defended an ethic of personhood that embodies an egoist-perfectionistic moral view, where the agent's greatest moral goal is her own self-realisation, which is understood in terms of developing a virtuous character. In this chapter, we gave an account of dignity associated with personhood, which explains it in terms of the capacity for sympathy. For the purposes of this book, I have stated that these are two different sides of the same moral coin, where we can appeal to the egoistic ethic of personal perfection or the ethic of dignity *qua* the capacity for dignity to resolve moral questions. The relationship that holds between the two sides of the moral coin of the ethic is available for a more systematic exposition and clarification. The essence of the relationship that holds between the two is — dignity *qua* the capacity for sympathy is foundational and the pursuit of moral perfection that involves the development of a sympathetic character is tantamount to leading a dignified human existence. In the chapters that follow, I appeal to both facets of the ethics of personhood — moral perfection and its view of dignity — to reflect philosophically on applied ethics. The idea is that the pursuit of personhood [dignified human existence] is reflective of our commitment to the idea of dignity [our capacity for sympathy].

Notes

1. I must caution the reader that I generally find the exposition of African languages [concepts] to be philosophically loaded and fruitful, as the reader will see in my treatment of some concepts in this book. I just do not believe this to be the case regarding the idea of dignity, particularly since it presupposes ethical supernaturalism.

2. Elsewhere, I offer a more extensive discussion of Ikuenobe's novel view of dignity and its criticisms (see Molefe 2019b, Chapter 6).

3. The idea of unconditional respect seems to be at home in a view that grounds dignity in merely possessing some ontological capacity. The respect is unconditional precisely because the agent, just being the thing that she is, is worthy of moral considerations. The moment one proposes, as does Ikuenobe, performance as a condition for dignity, it becomes difficult to retain the idea of *unconditional* respect.

4. This distinction is also captured in terms of 'honor', 'self-determination' (Brennan and Lo 2007, n.p.), 'full inherent dignity' and 'non-inherent dignity' (Michael 2014, 18).

3

Personhood and the equality of women in African philosophy

Introduction

In this chapter, I consider the place of women in the socio-political order imagined by the normative idea of personhood and its conception of dignity in African philosophy. Specifically, I aim to evaluate whether personhood — the patient-centred and agent-centred facets of it — intrinsically embodies a sexist and patriarchal socio-political order. I ask whether this concept takes women to be socially inferior, assigning them a secondary and marginal status in society. I hope the reader immediately appreciates why such a philosophical undertaking is important regarding the moral plausibility of the idea of personhood in relation to its implications and consequences for women in society. If, for example, it turns out to be *philosophically* true that the idea of personhood intrinsically embodies a moral-political theory that assigns an inferior status to women, that consideration alone will be reason enough for us to repudiate it. A plausible concept of personhood and its application to gender issues should have resources for a just social order. Such an order will characteristically be egalitarian — where women and men are treated as equals and equally.

In the final analysis, I will argue that the idea of personhood, correctly construed, has resources that can offer a robust socially egalitarian interpretation, where women and men are treated as social equals on the basis of a gender-neutral ontological feature that I will specify later.

To defend the view that the idea of personhood embodies a moral theory that requires that we organise social, cultural and political practice on the basis of equality, I will engage in a critical conversation with one of the leading scholars of personhood in African philosophy, Anthony Oyowe. In two essays, Oyowe (2013), and Oyowe and Olga Yurkivska (2014) argue that the idea of personhood is essentially inegalitarian or 'serve[s] a certain ideological function, viz. the perpetuation of patriarchy' (2014, 87).[1] I pursue my argument through the prism of Oyowe's philosophical views on personhood for several reasons.

Firstly, the very fact that Oyowe, in my view, is an authority on the discourse of personhood in African philosophy is reason enough. He has published a number of articles on personhood, which are, for the most part, in my view, very critical of it as a moral and political theory (see Oyowe 2013, 2014a, 2018. Secondly, the literature has tended to take implicitly the idea of egalitarianism to be a feature of the idea of personhood, without philosophical exposition and argumentation to secure this position (see Menkiti 1984, 178; see also Wiredu 2004, 2009). Oyowe's analysis of personhood is important because it argues the contrary — that the idea of personhood is not egalitarian — which position, if true, would amount to the conclusion that the idea of personhood, as a moral theory, is implausible and ought to be repudiated (see Oyowe 2013, 2018).

I think this philosophical engagement with the view advanced by Oyowe regarding personhood and its relationship to women provides an important philosophical opportunity to distil some of the moral-theoretical strengths or virtues of personhood as a 'communitarian model of ethics' (Oyowe and Yurkivska 2014, 86). The argument I will be advancing is that the idea of personhood does have moral resources to secure social-egalitarianism as a plausible conception of Afro-communitarianism. I will not, however, be asserting that this theory is the most plausible interpretation of egalitarianism *in toto* in moral philosophy; such a conclusion would be too ambitious at this stage. To secure that conclusion would require an extensively comparative and evaluative project, which is obviously beyond the scope of this limited chapter. The aim of this chapter is simply to tease out the theoretical elements of the ethics of personhood and to reveal its capacity to embody a just social order characterised by, among other things, gender equality.[2]

It is important for the reader to appreciate the fact that I do not dispute the empirical [sociological] considerations raised by Oyowe and Yurkivska regarding certain practices in African cultures (2014, 87). They observe that the actual make-up of African societies tends to be 'male dominated' and that the discipline of African philosophy in the academy is generally a 'male enterprise'. These empirical conditions are generally true, and earnest and consistent efforts to transform our institutions and societies are required. The dispute I raise is philosophical and theoretical in nature — the view that the idea of personhood can and does have resources to capture social egalitarianism (the equal worth of every human being), a view that Oyowe (2013) and Oyowe and Yurkivska (2014) negate.

Chapter 3

The question of the place of women in society is a crucial one to consider in Afro-communitarian ethics and its imagination of a just social organisation. Think of moral-political [applied ethics] issues related to women, such as gender-based violence, rape, human trafficking, cultural domination and exclusion, economic exclusion, and so on. Some of these practical problems facing women in our societies could be understood as an upshot of a socio-political order that considers women inferior. In fact, the problem might be deeper than just gender inequality, it could be rooted in the *dehumanising* culture of patriarchy that has been the order of the world until the recent past, if it is indeed a past problem. The standard of what it means to be 'human' in a patriarchal society is being a male. To be a non-male disqualifies one from the human project (Oyowe and Yurkivska, 2014). In this light, one of the reasons we ought to reflect on the place of women in African moral thought is to consider whether it does sponsor the dehumanisation of women in society. It is also important to appreciate that the problems that create the possibilities for the continued dehumanisation of women are structural ones.

I am highlighting these issues facing women in our societies, particularly in African societies, for two reasons. Firstly, I do so to suggest that the problem of the place of women in society is a moral-political question — it relates to the overall structure and governance of society. Secondly, I do so to argue that the idea of personhood (*ubuntu*) correctly construed does not sponsor the socio-structural conditions that dehumanise women (see, Oelofsen 2018). The suggestion will be that the idea of personhood imagines social relationships characterised by virtues of character and by dignity accounted for by appeal to the capacity for sympathy. The idea of dignity ought to inform how we structure our society in ways that recognise the equality of both genders.

To pursue this line of reasoning, I will begin by stating Oyowe and Yurkivska's view that interprets the communitarian idea of personhood as essentially sexist — an idea that perpetuates patriarchy and excludes women from the comity of equals in society. I take the essence of Oyowe and Yurkivska's argument, roughly stated, to revolve around the fact that personhood (as a moral view) is defined entirely in terms of social relationships. Their contention is that the concept of personhood tends to be construed in a way that overlooks the fact that the social relations that define it are characteristically unequal and take women to be secondary citizens. In the second section of the chapter, I will offer some responses to Oyowe and Yurkivska's criticism against personhood. I will proffer two responses. Firstly, I will insist that we distinguish between the ontological and normative concepts of personhood. I will point out that Mbiti's notion correctly understood is an ontological concept of personhood concerned with the question of personal identity. Secondly, I will insist that we need to argue from values to facts rather than from facts to values. Here, I will invoke a theory of moral status that informs the discourse of personhood, which should inform how we relate to each other, and to women specifically. I begin by discussing Oyowe and Yurkivska's view of personhood.

Oyowe and Yurkivska's on personhood

Below, I intend to discuss Oyowe's and Yurkivska's argument to support the view that the idea of personhood is essentially gendered, and that it imagines an inegalitarian social make-up. I will begin, however, by discussing how they construe the idea of personhood. Following this, I will proceed to consider their argument against personhood — particularly regarding its implications for women in society.

How do Oyowe and Yurkivska understand the communitarian normative idea of personhood in African philosophy? They begin by informing us that they derive the idea of personhood from leading scholars of the concept, specifically from Ifeanyi Menkiti and Kwasi Wiredu. Oyowe and Yurkivska understand this concept to be characterised by three features, namely: (1) its rootedness in community; (2) its processual nature; and (3) its normative component. Concerning its rootedness in community, the idea is that personhood is essentially defined in terms of being embedded in the community — I think reference to the community refers to the *cultural community*. The community (and all its cultural resources, structures and opportunities) is considered to be prior to the individual, and the life history of the individual is possible only in and through the community. Oyowe and Yurkivska (2014, 88–89) observe that the 'African view of personhood is a socio-centric view in which the status of an individual is determined through some socio-cultural criteria… persons are defined and individuated communally'. The upshot of this view is that an individual 'cannot be abstracted from the network of relationships by which she is defined…' (2014, 88–89). Put negatively, without social relationships personhood is not possible.

Concerning the processual nature of personhood, Oyowe and Yurkivska highlight the fact that personhood, in some sense, is *external* to the individual, and it is possible only by going through social stages. When the individual is born, she is, in some sense, not yet a person. Hence, it makes sense to think of personhood as somewhat external to the individual. By undergoing certain socially sanctioned and prescribed stages, the individual puts herself in the position where she can gain personhood. The upshot of this view is that being born is necessary but not sufficient for possessing personhood. Personhood is a function and consequence purely of responding positively to the socialisation process offered by the community to its members. Without the intervention of the community, the process of social transformation is impossible. The community, therefore, plays a decisive role in the social process of pursuing personhood.

Chapter 3

Regarding the normative dimension of personhood, Oyowe and Yurkivska (2014, 89) inform us that (moral) 'excellence is an indispensable part of African conceptions of personhood'. The individual, in this view, is required to internalise and exhibit 'certain values and excellences appropriate to personhood' (2014, 90). They further inform us that 'individuals attain personhood to the extent that they exhibit a sense of ethical maturity and conform to social rules…' (2014, 90). The essence of the normative facet of personhood seems to revolve around the quality of conduct that is exemplified in terms of how the agent relates to social roles and rules. To say that one is a person is tantamount to heaping them with moral praise for the quality of their moral performance.

Now that we have a sense of how Oyowe and Yurkivska (2014) define personhood, we can proceed to consider Oyowe's (2013) argument for the view that women occupy a secondary status in the personhood schema.

Oyowe's argument: Personhood, social power and egalitarianism

With this understanding of personhood from Oyowe in place, I believe we are in a better position to consider the substance of his argument. The essence of the argument marshalled by Oyowe regarding the idea of personhood and women pivots around two related facets: (1) its relational nature; and (2) the nature of the relations it invokes. The point that stands out is that personhood is essentially defined by appeal to social relations or cultural criteria. In this understanding, the very possibility of personhood is not imaginable or possible outside of the 'environing community' (Menkiti 1984, 171). In other words, the idea of personhood essentially requires continual embeddedness in a social structure for it to be possible. So far, so good. The problem begins when we consider the nature of the social relationships that characterise the idea of personhood. On this point, Oyowe makes two moves that are crucial to understanding the true character of the idea of personhood, at least in his reading of matters.

The first move connects the idea of personhood to that of the struggle for power in post-colonial Africa. The second move identifies that the social relationships that characterise the idea of personhood are anything but egalitarian in nature. I begin with the argument that the idea of personhood is essentially a struggle for power, and not an epistemic notion essentially involving plausibility.

Let us consider the relationship between the idea of personhood and social power. The context of this philosophical consideration is the *political* work the idea of personhood plays in the discourse of African philosophy. The function of the idea of personhood, we are told, is not a purely philosophical one; it does not essentially seek to show the logical validity or plausibility of the term. The idea of personhood emerges in a context of the political project of Africans attempting to culturally reaffirm their own identity, equality and difference against the insults of Western colonialism and imperialism. The concept of personhood is not so much about philosophical truth or plausibility, then, but rather the political goal of cultural affirmation against the onslaught of colonialism.

To demonstrate commitment to cultural affirmation via personhood is not to articulate a theory of personhood for the sake of truth, but for cultural ends. To make his case, Oyowe invokes John Mbiti's (1969) famous aphorism — 'I am because we are', which Mbiti understands as a cardinal view of personhood in African philosophy. This view stands in sharp contrast to Descartes's view that defines personhood in terms of an internal property — the capacity for rationality. The Western view defines personhood in terms of an internal property of human nature, while the African view defines it in terms of social relationships. After drawing this contrast between the two approaches of personhood, Oyowe proceeds to elucidate the major difference between them. He notes that Descartes' view is deductively valid (or could be rendered so if one understands it as an enthymeme). Oyowe observes that Mbiti's notion of personhood, however, fails the test of validity.

What is interesting for Oyowe regarding Mbiti's view of personhood is not the mere fact that it fails to meet the requirements of logic, but what we can read from this failure. Oyowe observes that despite Didier Kaphagawani (2004) demonstrating that Mbiti's conception of personhood is logically flawed, African scholars have insisted on it without attempting to defend its logical plausibility. According to Oyowe, this unrelenting commitment to an implausible view of personhood can be accounted for by the fact that the aim was never an epistemic one. It served some end other than philosophical truth. Oyowe captures this view as follows –

> Indeed, my submission is that the search for a unique and distinct theory of African personhood and the overall occupation with difference that characterises the often strident defense of the communitarian and normative conception betrays the same kind of motivation that spurred the articulation and defense of negritude and ethnophilosophy…the need for cultural reaffirmation of the African identity and a power struggle against the forces of imperialism. (2013, 210)

In light of the above, in Oyowe's view, the idea of personhood is engaged in a 'struggle for power' against colonialism, and the cultural desire to self-express and redeem one's cultural identity (Oyowe 2013, 243). However, the very culture that African scholars invoke to articulate the notion of personhood is loaded with power relations that essentially treat women as secondary citizens, or even non-citizens.

In light of the above interpretation, the idea of personhood is understood to essentially embody power relations. To get a clear picture of these power relations, we now have to consider the essential facet that defines personhood — the fact that it is definable entirely and strictly in terms of *actual* social relationships. While caught up in the struggle for cultural reaffirmation

> African communitarian philosophers lost the actual, embodied, inhabited, real persons because those are positioned and constructed in a fundamentally historical, culturally diversified, and gender-specific social realms. (Oyowe and Yurkivska 2014, 87)

This quotation brings several considerations to our attention. One consideration is that scholars of African thought and traditions have tended to theorise under the influence of a (gender) blind spot. It seems that they theorised without paying attention to the facts on the ground regarding, among other things, the position and conditions of women in African societies. Their focus was too centred on theory, to the point that they imagined or wished away the actual lived experience of women, and others. The actual reality on the ground is the fact that historically and culturally African societies tend to be gendered. That is, they distribute positions, power, roles and rules in ways that prioritise men and exclude women. Oyowe informs us that this view is supported by how Menkiti and Wiredu represent the idea of personhood in their philosophical work.

Menkiti represents personhood as related to age (seniority), social standing and class. He associates personhood with seniority. The older one is, the more of a moral exemplar one may be. The old and elderly are respected because they have epistemic access to truth, and exhibit mastery. This allows them (depending on their conduct) to earn respect in the community. So, the relationship between personhood and seniority is established in terms of age, which is a power relation. Remember also that personhood depends on one's social station, and how one performs in that position. Some positions, in the community, are better and more dignified than others, and those that do well in them will attract more attention and regard from society. Positions that are noble and dignified are the reserve of men. Another social factor that Oyowe points out to us is that of economic class, where the wealthy are respected more than the less wealthy. Often personhood is associated with a role that requires a man to pay lobola, get married and take care of his family (Wiredu 2008). Oyowe also points out the important role played by rituals and socialisation in the acquisition of personhood.

With regard to these facets that characterise the African social space, Oyowe makes the following remark –

> As it turns out, then, gender, seniority and social class represent multiple forms

of power relations that constitute social structure. Consequently, the concept of
personhood as socially engendered must rest on these modes of power relations.
Indeed, it seems impossible to construe this concept otherwise. (2013, 223)

In summary, the argument begins by asserting that the idea of personhood is definable strictly in terms of social or communal relations, or that it is essentially relational. It proceeds to perform an anthropological analysis of the actual social space in which individuals experience the pursuit and achievement of personhood. The actual social space of African societies is characterised by multiple power relations that manifest in the domain of gender, seniority, and social and economic status. The conclusion that follows is that the idea of personhood is not gender-neutral and does not embody the ideal of social egalitarianism — older, richer men are socially privileged. Thus, Oyowe observes that scholars of personhood would have 'a hard time explaining what it is about persons that make them morally equal' if the social structures that define the ideal of personhood are essentially not equalising (2013, 225).

The major criticism this argument makes against the idea of personhood is that it assumes social egalitarianism while 'the actual social conditions in which individuals find themselves' are fraught with all sorts of inequalities and injustices, gender being one of them (2013, 225). The idea of personhood can never embody social egalitarianism so long as it is defined by an appeal to social relationships that are essentially fraught with hierarchies and skewed power relations. From this analysis, the empirical considerations characterising much of the condition of African women should not come as a surprise. The fact is that politics in the continent is still dominated by males; major business corporations, universities, kingdoms, schools and so on are still (predominantly) led by males in a masculine culture. The conclusion is inevitable — the idea of personhood has no moral resources to offer an equal society in the truest sense of the term — where the opportunities in society are not determined on the basis of gender bias and hierarchies.

Personhood and social egalitarianism

Against this, in what follows, I aim to demonstrate that the idea of personhood, rightly construed, does actually have the resources to account for a just and gender-neutral, egalitarian society. To demonstrate this view, I will structure my argument as follows. I will begin by insisting that we need to draw a sharp distinction between the ontological and normative notions of personhood. This distinction is crucial since it will show us where a plausible theory is most profitably sought. Secondly, I will proceed to indicate that the normative idea of personhood has the resources to secure an equal and just society. The reader will do well to remember the dual features of the ethics of personhood. On the one hand, the idea of personhood requires agents and their social relationships to be characterised by the centrality of the idea of moral excellence. On the other hand, I will also point out that the idea of moral status associated with personhood embodies a gender-neutral egalitarian social order. Let us begin by considering the distinction between ontology and normativity regarding personhood in African philosophy.

Ontology or normativity?

One of the major limitations that attend Oyowe's characterisation of personhood, in my opinion, is that he does not carefully distinguish between the ontological and normative views, although he is aware of this distinction (see Oyowe 2014a, 2014b). The idea of personhood is ambiguous insofar as it could be a claim regarding certain facts related to being human or it could be making moral judgements regarding the human subject and her conduct in the moral sphere. One such fact relates to the idea of being a member of the *homo sapiens* species, which is hardly controversial. The more controversial fact relates to the assertion by Mbiti that 'I am because we are'. In Oyowe's view, this is a position that is philosophically implausible since, at heart, it is essentially a non-epistemic view aiming to affirm certain cultural ideals. I disagree with this reading of matters.

To successfully repudiate the view of personhood represented by Mbiti, one needs to do more than a simple logic test. One needs to appreciate and revisit the overall debate between liberals and communitarians regarding the correct conception of personhood in philosophy. Mbiti's assertion that 'I am because we are' is much more complicated than a mere contrast to the Western view for the sake of cultural reaffirmation, as Oyowe simplistically suggests. In my view, I charitably construe Mbiti as adding an African voice to the debate regarding how to define personhood *qua* personal identity using familiar Western modes of expression. The view that Mbiti is advocating, construed metaphysically, amounts to the position that scholars of African thought refuse to define personal identity without an essential reference to the ontological fact of the cultural community wherein individuals live. In this view (at least as presented by Mbiti and Menkiti), personal identity is definable entirely in terms of social relationships. Kwame Gyekye's (1992) and Michael Eze's (2009) interventions on this debate are decisive. They insist that the community does constitute personal identity, albeit partially.

The view that the idea of personhood captured in the expression 'I am because we are' has not received a defence in African philosophy is not true. I think Gyekye's (1992) essay does offer one of the strongest arguments for the view that personhood ontologically depends on the community. The ontological view under consideration is that personhood *qua* personal identity depends on cultural facts that are necessary for socialisation. Gyekye captures this view –

> It is an obvious fact, of course, that an individual human being is born into an existing human society and, therefore, into a human culture, the latter being a product of the former. As an Akan maxim has it, when a person descends from heaven, he descends into a human society (onipa firi soro besi a, obesi onipa kurom). The fact that a person is born into an existing community must suggest a conception of the person as a communitarian being by nature, even though some people insist on the individuality of the person. The communitarian conception of the person has some implications: it implies, (i) that the human person does not voluntarily choose to enter into human community, that is, that community life is not optional for any individual person; (ii) that the human person is at once a cultural being; (iii) that the human person cannot — perhaps must not — live in isolation from other persons; (iv) that the human person is naturally oriented toward other persons and must have relationships with them; (v) that social relationships are not contingent but necessary; and (vi) that, following from (iv) and (v), the person is constituted, but only partly, by the social relationships in which he necessarily finds himself. (1992, 105)

This is an instance where an African philosopher defends the view that 'I am because we are' or the idea that personhood *qua* personal identity depends on some ontological facts. The force of this argument is the premise that asserts that without and outside of culture, humanisation or socialisation is impossible. The idea advanced here is that being human, in terms of personal identity, is cultural by nature (see Wiredu 1996a). Furthermore, Gyekye insists that social relationships (or existing in groups) is natural to human beings since they are wired for relationships. Gyekye's argument differs from that of Mbiti and Menkiti in that it takes a moderate view regarding the role of the community in shaping personal identity by recognising a role for individual autonomy and creativity. The point, however, is to disprove the view that Mbiti's position on personhood has not been defended philosophically.

Moreover, the literature that considers the debate between individualistic and relational conceptions of personhood *qua* personal identity endorses the view defended by Mbiti and Menkiti (Neale and Paris 1990). The liberal view of personhood tends to define it by an appeal to some features internal to the individual, like memory, consciousness and so on. This feature is taken to be both necessary and sufficient for personal identity. A more charitable interpretation of the liberal view would not entirely rule out social relationships. It would simply assign them a contingent function and status. In other words, what ultimately accounts for personal identity are the ontological features internal to the individual (rationality, etc.) (Neale and Paris 1990). In this view of personal identity, the self is separable from social relationships, and, in the event of separation, the self is prior to them (Neale and Paris 1990). Descartes best demonstrates this separation when he doubts every form of relationship he has in and with the world until he remains with the crucial ontological feature that defines personal identity — the capacity to think (reason).

The communitarian view, on the other hand, insists that social relationships are essential in the constitution of the self, albeit partially (see Neale and Paris 1990). In this view, the self should not and cannot meaningfully separate from social relationships because they constitute an essential part of what defines it. Moreover, this debate has recently been joined by feminists who also emphasise social relationships in the constitution and functioning of the self, ontologically and morally. These feminists have centred the debate around the idea of autonomy, where they repudiate interpretations of autonomy that treat it as a property entirely within the locus of control of the individual (the 'in-control agent view of autonomy'). They (alongside some African scholars on the idea of personhood) insist that autonomy is a property that is nurtured and functions within social relationships, and they insist that we should understand it in relational terms (as 'relational autonomy') (see Gilligan 2002; Christman 2014; Ikuenobe 2015; Molefe 2019a, Chapter. 5).

In light of the literature from Western liberalism, African communitarianism and feminism, it is premature to simply dismiss Mbiti's view of personhood *qua* personal identity as controversial and illogical. In the light of insights from the communitarian and feminist contributions, Mbiti's assertion is open to interpretations that insist that personal identity is largely a function of being in a network of social relationships.

The reader should notice that above I have been discussing facts that relate to the debate regarding how to define personhood and the role of the cultural community. I have not referred to any *moral* values. It has been my observation that we should be able to separate the ontological notion of personhood *qua* personal identity from the normative one, which involves essential reference to the value of moral excellence or virtues (see Molefe 2016, 2018). It is also in keeping with my approach that when we characterise personal identity as requiring the cultural community for its realisation, we keep in mind that we are appealing to cultural values as opposed to moral ones. By 'cultural values' I have in mind things like how to dress, sing and dance, get married, educate, greet and court others (see Wiredu 2005, 2008). An African communitarian society has its own cultural values regarding how to socialise individuals in the quest of forming personal identity. I call these *cultural* values insofar as they emerge from a social context and can change over time, and some of them *ought* to change as the social circumstances and conditions permit and demand.

My view, however, is that for conceptual and substantive reasons, we need to separate moral from cultural issues. The major flaw in Oyowe's argument against personhood is that he wants to determine the status of a moral notion by considering factual anthropological or sociological considerations characterising African societies. Practitioners (be they philosophers or cultural experts) might be caught up in the contingencies of their own societies in their elaboration of the term, but that does not mean that the moral concept itself has no internal resources in offering a plausible *moral theory*. In my view, the function of philosophy and the philosopher is simply the ability to transcend these social contingencies in search of the truth (Jones 2001). This is a very serious consideration to recognise. It is possible that the idea of personhood has been used for non-epistemic ends, or as an expression of the struggle for power, and has been interpreted in ways that perpetuate patriarchy. To be cognisant of the use of personhood in ways that perpetuate patriarchy is not the same as claiming that the idea, in and of itself, has no moral resources for theorising about a just social order. Alternatively, it is not true to say that its use in responding to the colonial onslaught exhausts its moral career in the domain of African philosophy.

In what follows below, I consider the normative idea of personhood and its under-explored moral-theoretical possibilities for accounting for social justice.

Normative personhood

The third component of personhood, according to Oyowe, is moral excellence. The idea of personhood and its association with the value of excellence could be interpreted on two levels — a strictly cultural or a broader moral level. Oyowe seems to take a narrow interpretation of personhood, as does Gail Presbey (2002, 257), that reduces it to 'intragroup recognition'. This reduces personhood to strictly cultural norms and values of excellence. I propose that we should interpret the idea of personhood as embodying a trans-cultural system of values, or a moral theory in the fuller sense of the term. In this view, when we talk of an African concept of personhood, we are referring to a salient system of values inherent in African cultures that does not limit its moral application only to Africans, but to every human society insofar as it is a moral theory proper (see Chapter 2). By 'moral theory proper', I mean it is built on trans-cultural or objective values, which are necessary in order to conceptualise a robust society.

This approach to the discourse of personhood (that it embodies a moral theory) is suggested by a number of scholars. Notice, for example, that Thaddeus Metz (2007) in his search for a plausible interpretation of an African moral theory, includes the idea of personhood as one of the competing candidates. Concerning this view of morality, Metz makes the following comment — 'Many thinkers take the maxim "a person is a person through other persons" to be a call for an agent to develop her personhood' (2007, 331). Metz rightly suggests that 'this is probably the dominant interpretation of African ethics in the literature'. Another leading scholar of African philosophy, Kwame Gyekye (2010) notes that 'the concept of a person in African thought embodies ethical presuppositions', though he does not go on to unfold these.

Such ethical presumptions, Wiredu informs us, cover 'the entire sphere of human relations, the system of values presupposed cannot be anything short of an ethic' (Wiredu 2009, 15). We also know that the ethical system embodied by the idea of personhood is that of perfectionism or self-realisation, where the agent is required to perfect her own human nature (see Metz 2007, 331; Behrens 2013, 111; see also Chapter 2 of this book).

This idea of personhood embodies a moral system that is concerned with the character development of the agent (Van Niekerk 2007). The agent's deportment is expected to abound with and exude moral virtue. The virtues that ought to characterise the agent, for the most part, are other regarding. Note Gyekye's adumbrations regarding the nature of the virtues associated with the ideal of personhood –

> And because he is thought to be capable of displaying those virtues, it is expected that he would, when the situation arises, display them in his conduct and act in conformity with the accepted moral values and standards. Considering the situations in which that judgement is made about persons, these norms, ideals and moral virtues can be said to include *generosity, kindness, compassion, benevolence, respect and concern for others; in fine, any action or behavior that conduces to the promotion of the welfare of others*. And the reason for that judgment made of an individual is that that individual's actions and conduct are considered as falling short of the standards and ideals of personhood. (1992, 110; emphasis mine)

It is important to notice that Gyekye defines personhood in terms of moral virtues. I wish also for the reader to notice the kinds of values that he associates with the idea of personhood. These are other-regarding virtues like compassion, benevolence, respect and so on. In other words, the idea of personhood embodies virtues that throw the agent into robust social relationships, whereby the welfare of others is an important consideration. The reader should notice the kinds of social relationships imagined by the idea of personhood: it is those that are laden with moral virtues that are conducive to the welfare of others, by generating other-regarding duties.

We can draw out one crucial insight regarding the idea of personhood and the ideals it embodies for individuals and society. It imagines individuals whose most important moral responsibility is to perfect their own humanities, a moral task that requires them to relate positively to others. This positive relation to others imagines social connections attended by other-regarding duties of love, care, compassion, generosity, respect for others and promoting others' welfare (Gyekye 1992, 2004). This interpretation of the ideal of personhood begins to suggest that the idea of personhood imagines a society where all (moral patients) are treated with care and respect. This, in turn, begins to undermine Oyowe's criticism of personhood. The social relationships imagined by personhood are overwhelmingly characterised by virtues one would not naturally associate with the marginalisation of women (or any grouping) in the way Oyowe suggests. Let me turn, then, to a fuller consideration of the egalitarianism of the idea of personhood.

Personhood, moral status and social justice

Above, we considered the moral theory as imagined by the idea of personhood — a theory of virtue. The agent's chief moral goal, in this view, is to perfect her own character. Once perfected, it will be characterised by other-regarding virtues that are oriented towards creating a humane society (Kudadjie 1992). The crux of Oyowe's objection is that the idea of personhood is essentially inegalitarian in nature. This might be true if viewed from one angle, and false from another. This accusation of inegalitarianism is true in the sense that not everyone ends up achieving a virtuous character in society. It follows that some individuals will be more virtuous than others; some will be outright indifferent towards morality, and others morally bankrupt. As a result, we will have a society with some individuals doing well and deserving respect, and some less so. Below, I reveal the social egalitarianism associated with personhood.

To get to the egalitarianism of personhood, I urge the reader to remember the distinction between *recognition* and *appraisal* respect (Darwall 1977). The idea that some individuals might excel in the project of pursuing personhood is tantamount to appraisal respect, where the agent is respected relative to how well she does in the pursuit of moral excellence. The kind of respect imagined here is one that varies relative to the quality of performance; the measure of appraisal respect of the agent is proportionate to the excellence that attends her conduct. This is not the kind of respect that is important when thinking about questions of equal justice or egalitarianism; it is *recognition respect* that matters in the discourse of justice (Darwall 1977; Kymlicka 1990). This is the kind of respect that tracks the mere possession of the relevant ontological feature and is tantamount to the discourse on *moral status* (Toscano 2011). In this approach, we respect some entity merely because it possesses the relevant kind of ontological equipment or faculty.

Grounding respect in recognising certain facts about the nature of the respected entity is relevant to the discourse of social justice because it offers a robust way to think about equality. It also offers grounds to equalise individuals. I take the discourse on social justice to be centrally concerned with treating members of society as equals, or equally (Kymlicka 1990). With recognition respect, we respect individuals merely because they possess certain ontological features. Equal regard works perfectly through the lens of recognition respect because firstly, the individual does not achieve or earn these ontological features, and secondly, respect is a function of merely possessing the features in question. Hence, by merely being a possessor of the relevant features, one is owed moral regard or, more accurately, *equal* moral regard. Why must it be equal?

It must be equal because we respect beings in virtue of their possessing the relevant property rather than using it.

In what follows, we philosophically consider whether the idea of personhood entails a theory of moral status that can embody social egalitarianism. Such a theory must secure the equality of all members of the moral community, with a special focus on the question of women. A careful consideration of Menkiti's (1984) essay, I will argue, suggests such a promising gender egalitarian view.

I begin by submitting that Menkiti's idea of personhood suggests a particular theory of moral status — one where we respect some entity because it has the ontological material that matters for personhood to be possible. The idea of moral status emerges from Menkiti's adumbrations when he invokes John Rawls's idea of personhood as being close to the one that he finds to be salient in African philosophy — the idea that personhood is some kind of moral achievement. Menkiti (1984, 176) begins by noting a concept of personhood that is associated with justice, and which requires that we respect persons. The reader should remember that Menkiti discusses the idea of personhood as embodying an ethical sense from John Rawls's book, *Theory of Justice* (1971). The idea under consideration of a person is the patient-centred one, or moral status/dignity. In this view, personhood [moral status] is a function of being capable of a sense of justice or its potential. This view of moral status is endorsed by Rawls (1971, 505) when he states: 'The sufficient condition for equal justice [is] the capacity for moral personality'. In other words, we owe duties of justice — equal moral regard — to any entity that has the capacity for moral personality. Notice, the respect imagined here is recognition respect — we respect the individual because it possesses certain ontological capacities.

I hope it is obvious that the idea (of personhood) we are dealing with is that of moral status. Affording equal respect here involves recognising particular ontological features in the subject. In another passage, Menkiti (1984, 177) articulates the relationship between a view of moral status and rights, and its implications for animals. Menkiti begins by informing us that –

> If it is generally conceded, then, that persons are the sort of entities that are owed the duties of justice, it must also be allowed that each time we find an ascription of any of the various rights implied by these duties of justice, the conclusion naturally follows that the possessor of the rights in question cannot be other than a person. (1984, 177)

Again, Menkiti emphasises the view that persons *qua* those entities that have moral status are owed duties of justice. One way of showing moral respect of the recognitional kind involves assigning rights to persons. In Menkiti's view, duties of justice, which are captured in terms of rights ascriptions, are owed only to persons.

I stress that the idea of a person, as employed here, is not the same as employed under the rubric of moral achievement. This view is evidenced by what Menkiti says next; he informs us that 'such rights ascription has now been made dependent on a possession of a capacity for moral sense' (1984, 177). It is clear that duties of justice, expressed through an ascription of rights, are a function of possessing a capacity for moral sense. To clarify which ontological features qualify one as bearer of rights (a person), Menkiti proceeds to contrast persons to animals. He objects to the ascription of rights to animals because they do not possess the relevant ontological feature — a capacity for moral sense. He makes this point in the following fashion –

> The danger as I see it is that such an extension of moral language to the domain of animals is bound to undermine, sooner or later, *the clearness of our conception of what it means to be a person*. (1984, 177; emphasis mine)

The objection to the extension of rights to animals is predicated on the view that such a move will undermine our clear conception of what it means to be a person. The idea of personhood here is one that is related to rights ascription, the idea of moral status. Menkiti is also very clear that personhood, in his view, is a function of possessing the capacity for moral sense –

> …because the basis of such rights ascription has now been made dependent on a possession of a capacity for moral sense, a capacity, which though it need not be realized, is nonetheless made most evident by a concrete exercise of duties of justice towards others in the ongoing relationships of everyday life. (1984, 177)

The ontological feature that is necessary for some entity to be owed duties of justice or ascribed rights is the possession of the capacity for moral sense. To ground duties of social justice in the relevant capacity secures the equality of entities because it is based on an invariant capacity of human nature (Beitz 2009, 37; Tasioulas 2012, 669; Metz 2013a, 12). It is this fact that accounts for why these entities ought to be respected equally because the respect in question is not based on achievement or merit, but the mere possession of the relevant capacity.

It is not entirely clear what Menkiti has in mind when he talks of the capacity for moral sense. Perhaps the best way to decipher his meaning is to consider what he takes to be the goal of morality — the development and consistent manifestation of moral virtue (personhood). We can conclude, therefore, that the capacity that does the job of accounting for moral status, in terms of his normative theory of personhood, is related to virtue. That is, entities have moral status or are owed duties of justice because they have the capacity for virtue. Put more precisely, the agents are expected to pursue moral virtue (personhood) because they possess the ontological features that make it possible. The insight here captures the two sides related to the idea personhood as a moral theory: on the one hand, it embodies a theory that assigns respect to some agent relative to the quality of her conduct (appraisal respect); and, on the other, it assigns respect on the basis of the capacity for virtue (recognition respect).

This dual-featured reading of matters is an important contribution to the personhood literature. Scholars of African thought committed to the idea of personhood tend to appeal to different (metaphysical) considerations to ground dignity in African philosophy. One outstanding example of this tendency can be found shared in the works of Gyekye (1992) and Wiredu (1996). Gyekye considers the idea of personhood and the contribution it could make to thinking about a just society in his now famous view of moderate communitarianism. To articulate a theory of social justice *qua* moderate communitarianism, he is aware that the idea of moral status or dignity is indispensable. As a result, in articulating his theory of social justice, he offers three different (or even competing) views of dignity without trying to evaluate which is the most plausible: (1) he grounds it in the fact of being a child of God or the possession of the divine element of *okra*; (2) he grounds it in the possession of the *image of God*; and (3) he grounds it in the capacity for *autonomy*. The same is true with regards to Wiredu, who appeals to the metaphysical property of *okra* to ground human dignity.

These scholars are committed to the idea of personhood, but (at least on the surface) do not consider that it might embody its own conception of dignity. Gyekye, however, is more nuanced. He is aware, as highlighted in Chapter 2, of the intrinsic relationship between the idea of personhood as moral excellence (the agent-centred notion theory of value) and the capacity for moral virtue (the patient-centred theory of value). The patient-centred notion is a metaphysical concept that informs two sorts of moral considerations. Firstly, it explains how recognition respect is due to every human being for merely being human (at least for those human beings with the potential to develop this capacity for virtue). We owe unconditional respect to such beings. Secondly, it explains why we expect human beings to live morally upright lives — to pursue personhood. Note that the mere fact that human beings are wired with the possibility does not guarantee that they will pursue and achieve personhood. It is on the basis of their capacity for virtue [sympathy] alone that we can hold individuals morally responsible for their actions and conduct.

Direct response to Oyowe's criticisms

In light of the conception of moral status entailed by the idea of personhood, we are able to respond to Oyowe's criticism that personhood embodies an inegalitarian moral view that inferiorises or marginalises women in society. Remember, Oyowe (2013, 220) insists that 'a plausible theory of personhood should be able to explain why it is the case that we intuitively believe that all persons [human beings] are morally equal'.

Above, I articulated a theory of dignity *qua* the capacity for virtue [sympathy] that accounts for why we must consider all human moral patients to be morally equal. The capacity for virtue [sympathy], therefore, captures the egalitarianism of the idea of personhood. It is also important to notice that this view of dignity *qua* the capacity for virtue is gender-neutral. One has this feature by merely being human, before being socialised or acculturated.

The reader should remember that, in Chapter 2, I suggested that the capacity for virtue could equally be expressed in terms of the capacity for *sympathy*. In this case, sympathy is taken to be the root of all virtue. This view is reiterated by Kai Horsthemke (2018, 63) when he notes that 'sympathy and empathy, [are] both singled out by Wiredu as the "very foundation of morality"'.[3] I also take sympathy to be the very foundation of morality insofar as human beings, metaphysically speaking, are wired to be able to respond to others' needs and welfare. If this capacity is the foundation of all other virtues (morality), it follows that the central moral capacity that accounts for our ability to pursue personhood can be captured in terms of the capacity for sympathy. It is in virtue of possessing this capacity that all human beings have dignity and are owed equal moral respect.

It is worth noting that, if dignity in African philosophy is captured in terms of the capacity for sympathy, it is comparable to feminist accounts. It is important to notice also that Carol Gilligan (2013, 13) accounts for dignity in terms of the 'capacity to care' (13); 'capacity to love', or even the 'capacity for empathy' (22). What is important about both moral approaches is their emphasis on the point that social relationships are an organic (natural and essential) facet of human existence, ontologically and morally speaking. The aim of morality revolves around being embedded in these relationships, generating care or other-regarding virtues related to the quest of personhood.

The last aspect of Oyowe's criticism appeals to actual social relationships as a way of challenging the plausibility of personhood. Oyowe insists that personhood is acquired in social spaces that are defined by skewed social relations and, as a result, the moral view embodied in this concept cannot be egalitarian. The major flaw of this argument is that it embodies an incorrect theoretical approach. Personhood, as a concept, embodies moral ideals and values that *ought* to shape society and social relations. The actual social relations do not constitute the idea of personhood. The idea of personhood gives us two related ways to think about how to construct and reform social spaces in Africa and everywhere else.

Firstly, the social space must operate on the axiomatic moral principle of treating individuals equally. This ethical respect to treat members of society as equals is informed by the fact that they possess the capacity for sympathy. It is this capacity that accounts for why we as members of the moral-political community are equal and owed duties of justice. To have dignity has certain social implications for how we should treat individuals. One implication is that it imposes agent-centred restrictions (constraints) on the means we could use to pursue or maximise the good. In other words, it recognises the inviolability of each moral patient. Another is that it requires us, all things being equal, to aid moral patients when they require our help. In other words, the idea of dignity imposes general duties to aid beings of value. A further implication is that the idea of dignity requires that all beings that have it ought to be treated fairly and equally. By implication, if both men and women have dignity, it follows that we need a socio-political and economic system that will treat them equally (Jaworska and Tannenbaum 2018). The final implication is an emphasis on gender-neutrality and egalitarianism.

Secondly, the agent-centred idea of personhood informs us that we must relate to others in ways that are positive, or which enhance their welfare. In other words, individuals with personhood will exude other-regarding duties that tend to contribute to what Menkiti (1984, 181) refers to as the 'collectivity' (or, what Gyekye (1992, 1995, 1010) refers to as the 'common good'). The 'common good' refers to the exercise of the other-regrading duties that contribute to 'the provision [of] social conditions [that] will enable each individual person to function satisfactorily in a human society' (Gyekye 1992, 116). The duties associated with personhood aim to contribute to creating social conditions that enable each individual — without regard to gender or social class — to live an adequate human life. Thus, the idea of personhood embodies social values aimed at empowering individuals to live a decent human life. In Dismas Masolo's (2004, 494) view, the communitarian idea of personhood operates on the moral logic of the 'economy of affection', which I understand to encapsulate the idea of sympathy. This economy of affection requires '…that *everyone* should carry their share of responsibilities for creating humane conditions of life for everyone' (2004, 494; emphasis mine). The goal of other-regarding duties entailed by personhood has to do with creating social or humane conditions for everyone.

It is safe to conclude that both facets of personhood, as the patient-centred and agent-centred theories value, proffer a robust way of thinking about social justice. To ground dignity on the capacity for sympathy embodies social egalitarianism, and the idea of moral excellence requires that we create humane conditions for everyone, including the poor, the uneducated, women, children and so on. It is therefore not true that the idea of personhood lacks resources to account for the equal worth of every human being. It does so by recognising the fact that women have the capacity for sympathy, which secures them a place as equals in the moral-political community.

The two facets of the ethics of personhood — moral perfection and capacity for sympathy — ought to play a crucial role regarding the importance of culture and rituals in African societies. Those cultural practices, beliefs and rituals that do not lead to personal perfection or undermine such an ideal and those that do not recognise and enhance the individual capacity for sympathy ought to be revised or repudiated, depending on their nature. In other words, we may promote and support those cultural values that are neutral, or those that are consistent with the idea and ideals inherent in the value system embodied in the idea of personhood. As such, it is the idea of personhood that ought to regulate cultural beliefs and practices, and not the other way round.

Conclusion

In this chapter, I considered whether the idea of personhood does indeed have the resources to secure social egalitarianism and a vision of a humane society. I pursued this question in the light of the criticism raised by Oyowe and others that the idea of personhood perpetuates patriarchy and other forms of social inequality. I argued that the normative idea embodies a moral theory that requires agents to perfect themselves. This idea of personhood embodies other-regarding duties whose aim is to contribute to the common good, which requires agents to collaborate with others in the creation of humane social conditions. Furthermore, we noted that the idea of personhood is built on a particular conception of dignity *qua* the capacity for sympathy. This view of dignity is gender-neutral and equalises all human beings in terms of the duties of justice we owe to them. These arguments, in my view, are sufficient to disprove the view that the idea of personhood is not egalitarian. In fact, it has its own moral vision of a just society that operates on the logic of sympathy towards the lives and conditions of others.

Notes
1. I am aware of the criticism advanced by Manzini (2018) and Imafidon (2019) to the effect that the idea of personhood is essentially sexist insofar as it discriminates against women. I will be limiting my conversation to Oyowe because his argument covers most (if not all) of the concerns that they raise against the idea of personhood. This does not mean, however, that they contribute no insights of their own to the debate.
2. I am aware that Rianna Oelofsen (2018) pursues an argument that attempts to demonstrate that the idea of ubuntu does not subordinate women. Though we may reach more or less the same conclusion, we operate on the basis of a different interpretation of ubuntu. For her part, she relies on Metz's relational interpretation of ubuntu. In several of my writings, I have criticised this approach to the discourse of ubuntu. I hope this chapter offers another useful if not plausible way to secure the equality of women.
3. I am aware that Horsthemke uses both ideas of sympathy *and* empathy as the foundation of morality. This should not be surprising as Wiredu uses both too. Wiredu, however, seems to take these two terms to be interchangeable, which they might not necessarily be. Sympathy requires the agent to be able to relate to (or even identify with) another's

pain, whereas empathy requires that the agent also feels the other's suffering. It is for this reason that empathy might be taken to be too demanding. I do not agree with Wiredu's treatment of these two concepts as interchangeable. The reason I do not take sympathy to be interchangeable with empathy is that my understanding of African languages suggests that they do not have a term that captures the idea of empathy. The only term that features is that of sympathy: in isiZulu *uzwelo* and in seSotho *Kutlwelo bohloko*. These words simply mean the ability to feel for or identify with another.

4

The place of animals in African moral philosophy

Introduction

In this chapter, I consider the standing of animals in the moral-political community in light of African moral-political thought. I address the question whether we should acknowledge ourselves to have direct duties to animals. Another way to think of this issue is to deliberate whether we should consider animals to have rights. The discussion of animal rights is both a practical and theoretical project. There are various groups, in different parts of the world, agitating for animal rights. Theoretically, particularly in the West, there has been an intellectual drive to advance a case for such rights (Singer 2009). The case for animal rights, should it be theoretically sound, has serious implications for how we should reorganise ourselves as a human society. Some scholars compare this movement, in its practical and theoretical forms, to the struggles of women (women's liberation) and people of colour (civil rights movements in America) for liberation. Calls for the liberation of animals have been around for some time (Regan 1987; Singer 2009).

One of the leading advocates for animal rights, Tom Regan, speaks thus regarding this movement and its moral-political demands –

> I regard myself as an advocate of animal rights — as a part of the animal rights movement. That movement, as I conceive it, is committed to a number of goals, including: the total abolition of the use of animals in science; the total dissolution of commercial animal agriculture; the total elimination of commercial and sport hunting and trapping. (1987, 179)

Another influential advocate of animal rights, Peter Singer (2009), points out that the moral revolution in support of the liberation of animals will manifest in changes that ought to happen in our fridges, breakfast and dinner tables, forms of entertainment and so on. The animal rights movement calls for the total removal of animals from our diet as human beings, thus demanding the abolition of animal agriculture, and so

Chapter 4

on. The important question that arises in the light of these practical considerations is: how do these scholars ground animal rights morally and theoretically?

For his part, Singer grounds his call for animal liberation in his theory of moral status. His theory accounts for moral status by appeal to the animal's capacity to suffer and enjoy — its sentience. He says the following in this regard –

> What else is it that should trace the insuperable line? Is it the faculty of reason, or perhaps the faculty of discourse? But a full-grown horse or dog is beyond comparison a more rational, as well as a more conversable animal, than an infant of a day, or a week, or even a month, old. But suppose they were otherwise, what would it avail? The question is not, Can they reason? nor, Can they talk? but, Can they suffer? (Singer 1989, 152)

The central moral issue for determining moral status for Singer is not the ability to reason. The 'insuperable line' — the criterion for determining moral status — is whether the entity in question can suffer or not. Our discouragement of suffering and espousing of joy and happiness for humans should, on this account, apply also to animals. It should follow that any entity, including animals, that can suffer is owed moral duties.

For his part, Regan (1987, 186) grounds animal rights in the fact that animals are 'experiencing subjects of life'. Those entities that are subjects of a life insofar as they are conscious, sentient and can experience a variety of things going on in the world, have moral status. This view of moral status is individualistic insofar as it is grounded in some facet of the individual, regardless of whether it is a human being or an animal (May 2014). In this light, Regan (1987, 186) comments that – 'inherent value, then, belongs *equally* to those who are the experiencing subjects of a life…All who have inherent value have it *equally*, whether they be human animals or not.' In this view, animals have rights insofar as they are subjects of a life, and should be respected for their own sake. They have rights *equal* to any other entity that is a subject of a life.

Above, we offered a rough discussion of two differing strategies to secure the moral status of animals. On the one hand, it is secured by appeal to their sentience; on the other, it is based on their status as subjects of a life. I invoked the above practical and moral consideration regarding animals from the Western tradition to lay a platform for considering the moral status of animals in the light of personhood in the African tradition. To pursue the question of the standing of animals in the moral-political community, I structure this chapter as follows. I begin by defining the concepts of anthropocentrism and speciesism. I define these concepts because they are both crucial in the context of environmental ethics and, importantly, apply in the case of animals [animal ethics]. In the next section, I proceed to demonstrate the anthropocentric nature of much of the literature in African philosophy. I do so in two ways, namely: (1) by revisiting the writings of influential scholars of African philosophy (specifically, Kwasi Wiredu and Thaddeus Metz); and, (2) by considering this problem as it manifests in the idea of personhood (specifically in the adumbrations of Menkiti and Gyekye on animals). I will proceed to proffer an interpretation of personhood that can assign some moral status to animals. The essence of the argument that will be put forward is that animals have partial moral status since they can, at minimum, be objects of sympathy.

What is anthropocentrism?

I begin this section by defining anthropocentrism and I will proceed to consider the speciesism objection in the context of animal ethics. In the discourse of environmental ethics, the tendency is to distinguish between anthropocentric and non-anthropocentric views (Hargrove 2014). This distinction is crucial in environmental ethics because this field emerged, in part, as a response to the dominance of anthropocentrism, that is, theories of value that are human-centred (Behrens 2011). In this light, to label some approach or theory as *anthropocentric* is tantamount to the claim that it defines morality entirely in terms of human interests, or any other relevant property or benefit to human beings (Brennan and Lo 2016; Behrens 2010; Chemhuru 2016). The characteristic feature of anthropocentrism is the claim that human beings occupy a moral sphere that is privileged over or superior to any other living or non-living entities in the environment. The literature draws our attention to three distinct forms of anthropocentrism, namely: strong, weak, and enlightened anthropocentrism (Brennan and Lo 2016).

The defining feature of *strong anthropocentrism* is that it assigns moral value only to human beings. In this view, all facets of nature, including non-human animals, have no moral status at all. The upshot of this view is that the existence and presence of animals, in and of itself, does not occasion any moral issues or questions (Norton 1984). *Weak anthropocentrism* imposes a moral hierarchy between human beings and non-human animals, where the former occupy a higher moral sphere than the latter. The defining essence of this form of anthropocentrism is that, although it does assign intrinsic value to animals, it assigns a lower value than to human beings. In the case of a trade-off, human welfare will *always* be prioritised (Norton 1984; Brennan and Lo 2016). *Enlightened anthropocentrism* is generally characterised by some kind of moral pragmatism as an approach to questions and issues related to the environment. The approach here involves abandoning the search for a robust non-anthropocentric view. The general approach is to relate to the environment prudentially, for the sake of the future generations and for the benefit of human beings in general (Brennan and Lo 2016).

The central question we may wish to confront is — why should we be concerned about the question of animals in African philosophy? Alternatively, why should the question of animals be a serious one in relation to our traditional anthropocentric moral views? I think this question is important for moral and political theoretical reflection because it has the potential to reveal the blind spot of our moral views and theories, or to expose the overall limitation of our moral cultures. One of the central features of a robust moral theory is that it must be fair and consistent in its application of values, which implies that it must not be grounded in questionable biases or unjustified discriminations against other entities. If it turns out to be the case that our moral views exclude animals on the mere basis that they are not human beings, then we are encountering another form of an unjustified discrimination based on arbitrary ontological features. This kind of discrimination against animals simply because they are not human is classified in the literature as *speciesism* (O'Neill 1997).

The criticism against anthropocentricism is that traditional dominant theories of morality tend to be human-centred in a problematic form; they assume that morality must only be concerned with human beings. The typical structure of the arguments buttressing anthropocentrism is analogous to those that characterise racism and sexism (Singer 2009). Onora O'Neill (1997, 128) comments in this fashion regarding speciesism — 'The term *speciesism*, which was coined by analogue with terms such as *racism* or *chauvinism*, is usually used as a label for unjustified preference for the human species.' The mere fact that one is not white or is a woman does not offer sufficient 'reason' to discriminate or exclude one from the moral-political community. Thus, racism and male chauvinism are characterised by the unjustified preference for one's race or sex (Singer 2009; Horsthemke 2015).

The major problem with these kinds of 'arguments' for sexism (and racism) is that they cannot demonstrate what it is about being a male that is morally significant, or what it is about being a female that makes one morally inadequate. The property of being 'white' or being a 'male' is not a moral one. The same holds true for speciesism as it relates to the property or fact of being human in relation to animals. In and of itself, the property of being *non-human* has nothing to do with morality. The crucial moral questions should be whether the entity under consideration has the relevant capacities and/or whether moral agents can affect it in a way that makes a moral difference in terms of its life being better or worse off. If suffering, for example, is an important moral consideration when it comes to moral status (as it would be in a utilitarian account), then it should follow that our moral views ought to be able to accommodate the notion that all entities that can suffer have it [moral status]. To view the suffering of one entity, say a human being, as requiring urgent attention and relief above that of another, say an animal, is unjustified, particularly when the only relevant consideration is the fact of suffering itself.

In the light of the above, we note that the major reason we should be concerned about anthropocentrism in our moral-political discourse is the fact that it tends to be characterised by speciesism. The objection of speciesism, in my view, applies more to the cases of strong and enlightened anthropocentrism. This is the case because weak anthropocentrism assigns [some] intrinsic value to animals in their own right, and, as a result, treats them as deserving direct moral respect or rights (Norton 1984; Hargrove 2014). If I am correct that weak anthropocentrism is to be preferred over the other two forms of anthropocentrism, then it should follow that an account that at least embodies weak anthropocentrism is morally preferable. I set this low standard for our moral-political discourse because many moral commentators have observed that it is difficult to argue on the basis of a non-anthropocentric perspective to secure the moral status of many of the items environmentalists seek to include in the moral community (Norton 1984).[1] Later on in the chapter, I suggest that the idea of personhood embodies weak anthropocentrism, which grants animals a place in the moral-political community. Below, I consider anthropocentrism in African philosophy.

Anthropocentrism in African philosophy

For the sake of focus and due to limitations of space, I consider the instantiation of anthropocentrism in African philosophy in the writings of four scholars. I start with moral theories of two influential scholars of African moral thought, Wiredu and Metz; I then proceed to consider the writings of Menkiti and Gyekye as they relate to the question of animals in the light of personhood.

Wiredu's moral philosophy and animals

There is no doubt that Wiredu is one of the most influential African philosophers. He has written on a variety of philosophical themes in the African tradition, such as African culture, logic, metaphysics, and social and political philosophy (see Wiredu 1980, 1992, 1996a, 1996b, 2004, 2008, 2009). In what follows are his moral views and their implications for animals. To start, Wiredu (1980) observes that there are two meta-ethical options regarding the nature of moral properties in African moral thought; they are characterised either in secular (ethical naturalism) or in religious (ethical supernaturalism) terms. *Ethical-naturalism* accounts for moral properties in physical terms; it considers the source of ethics to be 'horizontal' (the natural or cultural world) (Pojman 2002; Wiredu 1992). Ethical supernaturalism invokes spiritual properties to account for morality; it considers the source of morality to be 'vertical' (the spiritual realm) (Pojman 2002; Molefe 2015b).

Wiredu is quick to repudiate ethical supernaturalism as the ground for a robust moral view. In fact, Wiredu (1996b, 234) states in no uncertain terms that – 'I deny that Akan moral thought is supernaturalistic to any extent' (1996b, 234). In fact, he espouses the view that ethical supernaturalist facets of African culture ought to be jettisoned since they are anachronistic (Wiredu 1980). For his part, Wiredu is unequivocal regarding his commitment to ethical naturalism. Familiarity with his moral philosophy will reveal beyond doubt that he espouses the view that African ethics is best construed in secular terms (1992, 1996a, 2004). He labels this meta-ethical view of ethical naturalism a *humanistic* approach to ethics (Wiredu 1992). This view is humanistic insofar as it accounts for morality in terms of some property of human nature. In other words, Wiredu can be construed to be either marrying morality to human nature or deriving morality from it (Molefe 2016).

He comments on this humanistic meta-ethics in this fashion — 'the first axiom of all Akan axiological thinking is that man or woman [humanity] is the measure of all value' (Wiredu 1996a, 65). Elsewhere, Wiredu (1992, 194) bases the articulation of his moral theory on the Akan assertion '*Onipa na ohia*' that embodies its entire axiology. Wiredu understands this assertion to amount to the following meta-ethical view –

> The word '(o)hia' in this context means both that which is of value and that which is needed. Through the first meaning the message is implied that *all value derives from human interests*. (1992, 194; emphasis mine)

From the above, it is indisputable that Wiredu reduces all morality to facts related to human beings, and human beings only. In fact, Wiredu informs us that all value derives from human beings, which I understand to imply that some facet of human nature is the source of morality. Wiredu is clear that 'human interests' encapsulate the entire project of morality, i.e morality essentially involves and revolves around human interests.

I believe that Wiredu's humanism implies, among other things, that animals have no moral standing at all (see Molefe 2015b, 2019d). This reading of Wiredu is true, I believe, because all value, for him, is derived only from human beings. The value of animals could, at best, be instrumental, which means they have value insofar as they are useful to advance human interests. The humanism advocated by Wiredu is dominant in African philosophy (see Gyekye 1995; Okeja 2013; Ikuenobe 2017). It is also important to see that since Wiredu reduces and limits all moral value to human beings, his views are characterised by the strong form of anthropocentrism. At best, in this view, animals matter only insofar as they are useful to human beings (see Molefe 2015b, 2016).

Metz on animals

At the heart of Metz's moral philosophy are relationships of *identity* and *solidarity* (see Metz 2007, 2010, 2011, 2012a, 2013b). Metz believes that these two relationships explain what African scholars have in mind when they speak of *community* or *harmonious relationships* as the highest good (Mokgoro 1998; Tutu 1999). The idea of identity encapsulates thinking of personal identity in terms of the reciprocal 'we', (1) where one imagines one's humanity in connection with others; (2) where those in social relationships share common goals, aims and aspirations; and (3) where they coordinate and collaborate to achieve their common goals (Metz 2007). More precisely, Metz describes the relationship of identity in terms of sharing a way of life with others (Metz 2013b). By solidarity, Metz is referring to caring relationships that promote the welfare of others for their own sake (Metz 2013b). The combination of these two relationships, according to Metz, offers a robust view of *ubuntu* as an African moral view, which can be reduced to the values of *friendship* or *love*, broadly construed (Metz 2007, 337). To say that someone has *ubuntu* is tantamount to saying that they are friendly or loving, in the sense captured by the twin social relationships of identity and solidarity (Metz 2011).

In his later writings, Metz extends this view to a theory of moral status or dignity. He terms his theory of moral status a *modal-relational view* (Metz 2012b). This view accounts for moral status in terms of the capacity to participate in the relationships of identity and solidarity. There are those entities that can participate in these relationships as both subjects and objects; and, there are those that can only participate as objects. Those entities that can participate in relationships of identity and solidarity as both subjects and objects have greater moral status or dignity. Those that can only do so as objects have partial moral status. In this view, normal adult human beings have dignity since they can participate in relationships of identity and solidarity both as subjects and as objects of such relationships. Animals, in Metz's view, can only be objects of the relationships of identity and solidarity, and therefore have partial moral status.

The above analysis of Metz's moral theory suggests that he advocates the weak form of anthropocentrism. I interpret his view as a weak form of anthropocentrism because it assigns animals some moral status. Metz affirms the anthropocentric nature of his moral view in this fashion –

> The theory might appear to be anthropocentric in that *it cashes out moral status in terms of certain human capacities*. To be able to be an object of a communal relationship, in this view, is analyzed in terms of a capacity to relate to normal human beings in a certain way. *And so there is an irreducible appeal to humanity in its conception of moral status.* (2012b, 399; emphasis mine)

Above, Metz makes several concessions regarding his moral view *qua* its status as anthropocentric. He informs us that it explains moral status in terms of certain human capacities. In other words, it is certain facts about being human and about our relation to animals that explains the moral status of animals. Insofar as animals can be harmed by unfriendly or unloving actions of human beings — insofar as they can be objects of certain human actions, that is — they have partial moral status. Metz also explicitly informs us that his theory of moral status has an irreducible appeal to humanity. What might we make of Metz's assertion that his moral view accounts for moral status by appeal to certain features of humanity?

I suggest that a careful analysis of Metz's modal-relational view would lead us to recognise that this theory embodies a *strong* form of anthropocentrism. I accuse Metz's theory of strong anthropocentrism since the moral standing of animals depends on their relation to human beings. Practically, the move to account for the standing of animals in terms of human beings makes sense given that it is human beings who pose the greatest threat to animals. I must hasten to add, however, that this move is *theoretically* inadequate. I provide the reason below.

I demonstrate the inadequacy of this theory to secure the moral standing of animals by appeal to the 'last man' objection (see Miller 2017). Does Metz's theory of moral status suggest that if the last man dies then animals will have no moral status or value in their own right, given that moral value is irreducibly human-centred-and-derived? I think this is the implication of Metz's view. It implies that the value of animals depends on the presence of human beings and disappears with them. Remember, animals have moral status because the human relations of identity and solidarity can affect them. If human beings are no longer present, it should follow that animals have no value, or that there is no way to make sense of their value because it essentially requires human presence. If they do have value in the absence of human beings, it is not clear what its source would be. I clarify this concern below by drawing from this hypothetical case.

Imagine aliens who are like human beings in every way except that they are not human. If Metz's theory of moral status is irreducibly human, it implies that although these aliens have the property that grounds moral status — the capacity for love — they nonetheless lack moral status for being non-human. It is not clear what the property of being human is *doing* that has moral significance, but it is essential on the modal relational view. Metz's view, implausibly, implies that although these aliens can harm animals, it would not count as doing something wrong because the moral status of animals emerges only in relation to human beings. I believe that the above demonstrates that Metz's theory is strongly anthropocentric, and thus speciesist, or implies that animals have no value (see Molefe 2017a). If animals had value in their own right then it should not matter who can harm them, whether human or not, as long as they are moral agents. But, if an account for moral status is essentially grounded in a human capacity *qua* human then it would arbitrarily exclude aliens and animals from the moral community.

Above, I briefly considered Wiredu's and Metz's moral theories. I argued to the effect that both of them embody a strong form of anthropocentrism since they base all morality on human nature in a way that is objectionably speciesist. Below, I consider Menkiti's and Gyekye's views on animals in the light of the idea of personhood. Their views also tend towards strong anthropocentrism.

Menkiti, personhood and animals

In his famous essay on personhood, Menkiti reflects on the question of animal rights. I cite from this essay at length because it gives us a clear sense of Menkiti's view of animals –

> The foregoing interpretation would incidentally rule out, I believe, some dangerous tendencies currently fashionable in some philosophical circles of ascribing rights to animals. The danger as I see it is that such an extension of moral language to the domain of animals is bound to undermine, sooner or later, the clearness of our conception of what it means to be a person. The practical consequences are also something for us to worry about. For if there is legitimacy in ascribing rights to animals then human beings could come to be compelled to share resources with them. In such a situation, for instance, the various governmental programs designed to eradicate poverty in the inner cities of the United States could conceivably come under fire from the United Animal Lovers of America, or some other such group, with the claim seriously being lodged that everything was being done for the poor, but not enough for the *equa*lly deserving cats and dogs. Minority persons might then find themselves the victims of a peculiar philosophy in which the constitutive elements in the definition of human personhood have become blurred through unwarranted extensions to non-human entities. (1984, 177)

Several considerations stand out from this quotation. Firstly, Menkiti believes that in his essay he has offered a plausible theory of moral status that settles the view that animals have no rights at all. If this reading of Menkiti is correct, it implies that his view espouses strong anthropocentrism. I will consider the reasons he gives for the rejection of animal rights below. Another thing that stands out is that Menkiti finds movements and theories that seek to defend animals to be entertaining 'dangerous tendencies'. The idea that animals have rights is dangerous, for him, because it creates a platform where human beings will have to compete or share resources with animals. The suggestion behind Menkiti's view seems to be that the interests of human beings should trump all interests of animals. Or, that the interests of animals should never arise at all when considering the resources required by human beings. He believes that the exclusion of animals from accessing crucial resources for welfare is based on a sound philosophical case.

The case he makes against what he refers to as a peculiar philosophy — the idea that animals have rights — is that it deviates from the clearness of our conception of what it means to be a person. The idea of personhood under consideration, here, should be rightly construed to refer to the idea of moral status (see Chapter 2). Then we may need to ask ourselves — what is the view of moral status that Menkiti is invoking to dismiss animal rights? Menkiti accounts for moral status by appeal to the capacity for moral sense. He is unequivocal regarding the view of personhood *qua* moral status that informs his views towards animals –

> [Since] persons are the sort of entities that are owed the duties of justice, it must also be allowed that each time we find an ascription of any of the various rights implied by these duties of justice, the conclusion naturally follows that the possessor of the rights in question cannot be other than a person. (1984, 177)

From the above, it is clear that the idea of personhood under consideration is that of moral status. He associates personhood with duties of justice. He also associates personhood with rights ascription. He then proceeds to inform us that 'rights ascription has now been made dependent on a possession of a capacity for moral sense' (1984, 177). Hence, in Menkiti's view, moral status is a function of the capacity for moral sense. For him, since animals do not have the capacity for moral sense or are not moral agents (lacking the ability to pursue personhood (moral perfection)), they do not have moral status. The upshot of the fact that animals do not have the capacity required to pursue personhood — the capacity for moral sense — is that they do not have rights. We can rightly conclude that Menkiti offers an interpretation of personhood that espouses a strong form of anthropocentrism.

Gyekye, personhood and animals

Like Menkiti, Gyekye rejects animal rights. Gyekye expresses the view that animals have no rights in this fashion (the reader should note that he does not use the language of rights) –

> The foregoing discussion of some morally significant expressions in the Akan language or judgements made about the conduct of persons suggests a conception of moral personhood; a person is defined in terms of moral *qualities* or capacities: a human person is a being who has a moral sense and is capable of making moral judgments. This conception of a person, however, must not be considered as eliminating or writing off children or infants as persons even though they are not (yet) considered as moral agents, as capable of exercising moral sense. The reason is that even though children are not morally capable in actuality, they are morally capable in potentiality. *Unlike the colt which will never come to possess a moral sense even if it grew into an adult (horse)*, children do grow to become *moral* agents on reaching adolescence: at this stage they are capable of exercising their moral sense and thus of making moral judgments. (1992, 111; emphasis mine)

In the previous chapter, I considered this quotation for the purposes of demonstrating that the idea of personhood (moral virtue) entails a particular conception of moral personhood (moral status). Gyekye accounts for moral status in terms of our capacity for moral sense and ability to make moral judgements. I hope by now that the connection between personhood *qua* moral virtue and personhood *qua* moral status is obvious. The connection is that those that have moral status *qua* moral *qua*lities or capacities for moral sense, choice and action can be expected to pursue moral perfection. After accounting for moral status in terms of these moral *qua*lities or capacities of human nature, it immediately occurs to Gyekye that his view might be construed to entail the moral consequence of excluding children from the moral-political community. Gyekye is aware that African cultures operate on the moral intuition that children do have moral status. He then recognises the need to offer an interpretation of moral status that can accommodate children.

To accommodate them, he amends his theory so that the minimum threshold for moral status becomes the mere potential for moral virtue. The result of this amendment is that only entities that have the potential for moral virtue have moral status. Since children, at least the normal ones, have the potential for moral virtue, it logically follows that they also have moral status. The implication of Gyekye's view is that normal adult human beings have full moral status or dignity since they possess the capacity for moral sense, or what, in the previous chapter, I captured in terms of the capacity for sympathy. Children, on the other hand, since they only possess the *potential* for moral sense, have partial moral status. We can now ask the question about the moral standing of animals.

What makes all the moral difference regarding whether one has or does not have moral status revolves around whether the entity in question has the relevant potential or not. Regarding children, it is obvious that they have the relevant potential. But regarding animals, it occurs that they lack the relevant potential. In clearer terms, Gyekye could be understood to be arguing that beings that will in future be able to pursue personhood (moral perfection) have moral status. Children have this potential, but animals have no potential for moral sense. Gyekye's argument could be construed to amount to the view that beings with the potential for moral virtue have partial moral status, and beings that will never be able to pursue personhood (due to deficient capacities or their nature) do not have moral status. In other words, given that animals will never be able to pursue moral perfection, because they lack the relevant moral *qua*lities or capacities, they do not have moral status. This lack of the capacity for moral virtue means that in terms of Gyekye's moral-political philosophy we can never speak of animal rights. Animals are totally excluded from the moral-political community.

Chapter 4

Rethinking personhood's application to animals

It is a commonly accepted view that African moral ideas tend to be anthropocentric (Behrens 2011; Horsthemke 2015; Chemhuru 2016). Specifically, the idea of *ubuntu*/personhood, in its various interpretations, and in its interpretation as a self-realisation approach (moral perfection) has been accused of being anthropocentric. I have already explored the evidence that sustains this accusation, above. Horsthemke makes the following remarks regarding African cultures and animal rights –

> Through exploration of what kind of moral status is reserved for other-than-human animals in African ethics, I argued in my recent book [*Animals and African Ethics*, 2015]…that moral perceptions, attitudes and practices on the African continent have tended to be resolutely anthropocentric, or human-centred. Although values like *ubuntu* (humanness) and *ukama* (relationality) have, in recent years, been expanded to include non-human nature, animals characteristically have no rights, and human duties to them are almost exclusively 'indirect'. (2018, 64)

In his book, *Animals and African Ethics*, Horsthemke (2015) explores various facets of African ethics, cultures, mores, taboos and so on. He concludes that African moral theories and cultural practices are resolutely anthropocentric. Horsthemke (2018) notes that the idea of personhood featuring in Menkiti's and Gyekye's writings is morally flawed insofar as it is, on the one hand, too narrow, and, on the other, too broad. It is too narrow insofar as it excludes young children, marginal cases, women, homosexuals and animals, among others, from the moral community; and it is too broad insofar as it includes ancestors. Hence, the idea of personhood, according to Horsthemke, is implausible at least because it fails to accommodate animals in the moral community.

Horsthemke finds the failure to take animal rights seriously to be concerning and surprising given the brutal history African countries have been subjected to. He makes the following comment regarding this history –

> Taking into account the brutal and dehumanising ravages of colonialism, racism and political, cultural and moral apartheid that Africans have historically been subjected to, it does not seem to be wholly off the mark to invite people in sub-Saharan Africa, especially, to reflect on an even longer, more deeply-entrenched historical process of discrimination, oppression and exploitation, namely that of species apartheid. (2018, 239)

The crux of the moral-political concern raised here is that African cultures and scholars should be more open. They should be careful to avoid moral myopia and parochialism of a kind similar to racism, colonialism and apartheid. The anthropocentrism associated with much of African moral thought embodies what

Horsthemke refers to as 'species-apartheid'. If this accusation is true, as the evidence explored above suggests in the case of Wiredu's and Metz's moral philosophy, then it seems that African people — given their history of oppression and suffering — have an especially strong moral basis to reconsider their attitude and moral views towards animals. Doing so would aid them in going beyond implausible forms of anthropocentrism, specifically the strong and enlightened versions of it that deny animals moral status altogether.

The central concern I seek to address, in the light of the overwhelming evidence that the discourse on personhood is anthropocentric, is to explore a *weakly* anthropocentric interpretation of it as a way to espouse animal ethics. The reader should remember that I stated that one virtue of weak anthropocentrism is that it does assign intrinsic value to animals, albeit not one equivalent to that assigned to normal, adult human beings. Thus, weak anthropocentrism offers a space for animals in the moral community. As a result, if a theory would prove to be weakly anthropocentric, at the very least, it would evade the 'species-apartheid' criticism. I suggest such an interpretation of personhood below.

The reader will do well to remember that the idea of personhood bases moral status, at the very least, on the potential to pursue personhood. That is, those entities that in future will be able to pursue personhood have partial moral status, and those that can actually pursue personhood have full moral status (dignity). The reader will also remember that we reduced the relevant property for moral status to the potential or actual capacity for moral virtue (sympathy). On this rendition of African moral thought, we still cannot secure the moral status of animals because they do not have the relevant potential.

I suggest that to accommodate animals, we need to further amend our theory of moral status. This amendment is motivated by the possibilities availed by the idea of moral virtue and/or sympathy. The highest moral goal posited by personhood is for the agent to be sympathetic, that is, to be morally sensitive and responsive to the suffering and plight of others. It would be morally myopic to limit the scope of the 'others' to human beings only, given that suffering is not limited to them. The view that we need to extend the scope of our sympathies to animals, for example, is suggested in the analogy of *hearing*, characteristic of the idea of sympathy in African languages. The human capacity to 'hear' — to be sympathetic — is attuned to the voice of the other, broadly understood. The hearing ear does not limit itself to the sound of the voice of other human beings only; it will also pick up the sound of anything that has a voice. It would be a mischaracterisation of the function of the ear to consider it capable of hearing only the voices of other human beings — the ear does not discriminate in this way. Similarly, the human capacity to be sensitive and responsive to the suffering of 'others' should not be limited to human beings only, but should be extended to include non-human animals also. It is human prejudice that limits the hearing moral ear only to the human voice. The challenge posed by this moral view is that we ought to overcome these prejudices by extending our moral sensitivities to include all sentient beings.

In the light of the above, I suggest that if we take sympathy as the final good of morality, it would extend the scope of our moral concerns beyond the potential for moral perfection. At a minimum, it would include many sentient beings in the moral community, although they cannot pursue personhood. They are included because they can be *objects of sympathy*. The logic here is simple, at least in my view. If the highest good is sympathy, then this highest good must not be limited to human beings; it must do good wherever it can. If the sympathy of human beings can do well for animals and the withholding of such a virtue can harm them, it follows that animals morally matter insofar as they can be objects of sympathy. The reader will notice that, here, I am employing the strategy employed by Metz, where I distinguish between entities that can be subjects and objects of moral perfection (full moral status) and those that can largely be objects of moral perfection (partial moral status). If this interpretation of moral status in the light of those entities that can be subjects and those that can be objects is correct, it follows that it assigns animals some moral status.

I do not hold the view that animals cannot manifest varying traces of sympathy. In fact, I espouse the view on empirical consideration that animals do manifest varying degrees or traces of sympathy. The very fact that most animals look after their offspring and group suggests traces of this capacity. To that extent, they can be 'subjects' of sympathy. I believe that this capacity is limited, however, to the extent that it cannot manifest in what would be properly labelled as personhood in the fullest sense of the term, where animals would exude moral perfection. Since animals are largely objects of sympathy, we can grant them partial moral status. If the argument marshalled here to secure the partial moral status of animals is plausible, it is because it embodies a weakly anthropocentric view.

This kind of inclusion of animals, I believe, is an important addition to the literature. Certainly, those scholars who aim for a purely non-anthropocentric view to accommodate animals will not be happy with such a view (Horsthemke 2017). However, it will work for most of those that believe that the sentience of animals ought to count for something. For my part, I am satisfied with this view insofar as it eschews the objections of 'species-apartheid' and speciesism, and grants animals some intrinsic value.

One objection against the view of moral status advocated here could be that if I assign moral status to animals on the basis that they are largely objects of sympathy then it should also be available to the same criticisms that I levelled against Metz's modal relational view. I do not believe this to be the case. Firstly, the view I defend assigns moral status on the capacity to pursue personhood *qua* capacity without tethering it to human nature in the way Metz's relational modal view does. It is the fact of possessing certain capacities for virtue *qua* capacities that accounts for moral status. In this light, it is a contingent fact that human beings happen to possess this property. By implication, if the alien has the capacity to pursue personhood — capacity for sympathy — then it does have full moral status, and does have duties to all sentient beings including animals. In this sense, my view is not speceistic like that of Metz, in that it does not account for moral status in terms of human capacities.

The major difference between the view of advocated here and Metz's view is that I believe my view to embody a weak version of anthropocentrism and I have demonstrated that Metz's modal relational view embodies strong anthropocentrism. The alien with the relevant ontological capacities has moral status and owes duties to animals. Not so, according to modal relationalism. In my view, the sentience of animals is sufficient grounds for creating duties for aliens. This is not so in Metz's modal relational view; aliens must first be able to relate with human beings before they can have morally relevant consequences towards animals. Hence, I find modal relationalism objectionable.

Another objection that can be raised against my view is that it is resolutely anthropocentric insofar as it insists that the capacity for pursuing personhood is the basis for moral status. I have already conceded, in some way, to this kind of objection, but I must hasten to clarify that this view embodies a weakly anthropocentric interpretation of moral status. It is not the fact of being human that accounts for moral status per se. Rather, it is the fact that human beings so happen to possess the relevant capacity that matters — the capacity for sympathy. In that light, it is more accurate to describe this view, not as resolutely anthropocentric, but rather as weakly anthropocentric. The virtue of such a view is that it does assign animals some intrinsic value, and this allows us to speak about animal rights. It is important to realise the moral-political potency of a weakly anthropocentric view. At most, it allows for prioritising human beings only in instances of a trade-off. For example, in a situation where I must drive over either a cat or normal adult human being, it would recommend that I drive over the former because it has less moral status than the latter. It is important to appreciate the fact that many of the harms suffered by animals today are not because of such trade-offs. They are a function of moral blindness and speciesism, which needs to be redressed.

It is also crucial to appreciate the fact that, in his criticism of African moral thought for anthropocentrism, Horsthemke (2017) expresses a hope that it does have non-anthropocentric resources to account for the moral status of non-human animals. He rejects the concepts of ubuntu, personhood and vitality for being resolutely anthropocentric (2017). He does not, however, suggest what axiological resources could be invoked in the African tradition of philosophy to secure such a non-anthropocentric view. For my part, I am satisfied that the weakly anthropocentric view associated with personhood does the work of securing a promising account of animal ethics. I am not yet convinced that we need a non-anthropocentric view to have a robust animal ethics in African moral philosophy.

Conclusion

The world is slowly moving towards a new moral conscientiousness, where animals are recognised as legitimate members of the moral-political community on the basis of moral reasoning. This movement has been calling for the recognition of animal rights in our moral, jurisprudential, and legislative infrastructure. In this chapter, I suggested one way to interpret the idea of personhood consistently with the call for animal rights. I suggested that a weakly anthropocentric view provides an avenue to espouse a meaningful way to engage in the practice and discourse of animal rights. The suggestion is that animals have a place in the moral-political community because they are objects of sympathy. This view does not mean that animals do not evidence traces of sympathy. Furthermore, it does not suggest that animals are not subjects in their own rights insofar as they are bearers of a variety of experiences. It simply points to their limitations regarding the moral experience, given that they cannot pursue moral perfection.

Above, three goals of the animal rights movement identified by Regan were mentioned, namely: (1) the total abolition of the use of animals in science; (2) the total dissolution of commercial animal agriculture; and (3) the total elimination of commercial and sport hunting and trapping. I am not yet sure that the weakly anthropocentric view associated with personhood in this chapter would totally abolish the use of animals in science, particularly in cases where it would add value to the lives of both animals and human beings. The use of animals in science should be on the understanding that animals have *some* moral status. This still requires careful analysis. I am sure, however, that the view advocated here would insist on the total abolition of commercial farming and the use of animals for hunting and entertainment. These activities reduce animals to 'things' that are useful merely for the use [consumption] and entertainment of human beings — 'things' that do not occasion value in their own right.

Notes

1 Space does not allow me to justify fully the view that weak anthropocentrism is the best option available, and that it can provide us with both plausible moral views regarding animals and practical policies regarding how we should relate to the environment. It is important to note that a number of scholars have argued (truly, I believe) that non-anthropocentric theories tend to collapse to weak anthropocentrism, or when they succeed, they entail an impractical moral theory (see Hargrove 2014; Keurlatz 2012). Take, as an example, the biocentric view that assigns moral status to every living thing. What this view essentially entails is that we have duties towards human beings, animals, bacteria, viruses and so on. With regards to bacteria, it becomes too difficult to know how not to harm them — such a theory is too inclusive and burdensome in its recommendations.

5

Personhood and development in African philosophy

Introduction

This chapter aims to articulate an African conception of development.[1] I label the view of development defended here 'African' insofar as it draws from the moral idea of personhood, which is salient among most African cultures (Masolo 2010). I pursue the theme of development motivated by three considerations. Firstly, it is a common view that the idea of development is an essentially contested one (Collier, Hidalgo, and Maciuceanu 2006). To classify a concept as *essentially contested* is to appreciate the fact that there is no standing agreement regarding its definition and its possible interpretations (or conceptions) in the literature. In this light, this chapter proffers one useful way to construe this concept in the light of personhood, a moral view indigenous among African cultures. In this I join a group of scholars of African thought that believe in the possibility of a robust African conception of development (see Kudadjie 1992; Dei 2000; Keita 2004; Asabere-ameyaw, Anamuah-Mensah, Dei, and Raheem 2014; Segage 2018).

Secondly, it is possible that some scholars must insist that we (scholars of African thought) should jettison the discourse on development altogether because it is reflective of the unending pursuit of the West to maintain its stranglehold on the economies and political futures of Africa. The suggestion is that we need to use novel categories to think about what Africa and its social, political and economic direction should be, without appeal to this idea (see Rahnema 1997; Matthew 2004; Ziai 2007). Metz (2017) argues that we need to abandon the idea of development in an essay titled — *Replacing Development: An Afro-Communal Perspective on Global Justice*. His major concerns is that the idea of development is too anthropocentric, too individualistic and too technocratic (see Metz 2017, 128–136). The strength of this rejection of the entire discourse of development is reinforced by considering some of the approaches to it that have been imposed on the African continent.

As an example of an approach to development that has been imposed on Africa, I draw the attention of the reader to the so-called *modernisation* discourse of development of the 1950s (see Davids, Theron, and Maphunye 2009). The major drawback of this approach is that it construes development in terms imported from Euro-American countries. It assumes that development is a linear process that can be transplanted from one part of the world to another (Vale and Maseko 1998). The reader would also do well to remember the disastrous adjustment programmes that came with the Washington consensus and the post-Washington consensus (Mkhandawire and Soludo 1999). These are surely examples of the wrong way to approach the discourse on development. The major problem with these approaches is that they overlook deep socio-political and economic structures that have created the underdevelopment of Africa (see Amin 1972). Furthermore, they assume that the resources to think about and approach development in Africa are inherent in Western cultures.

The third consideration that animated and motivated my pursuit of the theme of development is that it is dominated by approaches to it that tend to assume economism as the only way to conceive of development (Fine 2009). 'Economism' is the view that development is entirely an economic issue, usually reduced to economic growth and typically associated with profit-maximisation, taking pride of place in socioeconomic and political organisation (see Ajei 2007; Fine 2009; Ramose 2010). In this chapter, I pursue a conception of development that is rooted in African cultural and moral values, which will give us an African perspective of development.

This chapter proposes two useful ways to articulate an African conception of development. Firstly, it draws from African axiological resources to account for development. That is, it seeks to ground a conception of development in some salient strands of African culture(s), specifically the moral idea of personhood. I draw from African cultures because 'cultural resource base and knowledge of local peoples have been least analysed for their contribution to African development' (Dei 2000, 71). In other words, I employ the idea of personhood because not much philosophical work has gone into its implications for the discourse on development. I draw from African axiological resources of personhood informed by the view that '…for local people, indigenous ways of acting, feeling, knowing, and making sense of the social and natural worlds *have significant implications for development*' (Dei 2000, 31; emphasis mine). In the light of the above, I believe that the ethical idea of personhood provides us with the possibility of a 'homegrown paradigm for Africa's development' (Ajei 2007, 194).

Secondly, this chapter adopts an approach to the discourse on development that treats this concept as a moral one. The approach assumed here insists on the view that '…moral development is a *sine qua non* of all development' (Kudadjie 1992, 208). The view here is that development essentially revolves around 'the cultivation of [moral] values' among individuals that ought to be reflected in the crucial institutions of a society (Kudadjie 1992, 208). Not only is the idea of development anticipated a value-laden one, but it places the pride of place on the 'human factor' in development and it understands it to be 'total' insofar as it recognises the 'intimate understanding… of the relationship between humans, society and nature' (Kudadjie 1992, 210; Dei 2000, 76).

To effect the goal of proffering an African conception of development that is accommodative of the human factor and the centrality of African indigenous moral values, and that appreciates the relationship between the human, society and nature, I will adopt *development ethics* as a robust framework within which to contemplate development. I adopt this approach largely because, it treats development as a moral enterprise in a way that is consistent with (some of) our moral intuitions and (political) goals regarding the pursuit of the ideal of development. One salient moral intuition is captured in this fashion –

> When development programs are preoccupied with economic development, there is danger of losing that component of development that our forefathers fostered: real humanity, humaneness, fellow-feeling, and concern for one another. (Kudadjie 1992, 208)

Drawing from some African cultures, Kudadjie articulates two crucial considerations relating to development. Firstly, he contests attempts to reduce development to economic growth, what I referred to above as economism. Secondly, he construes development as being centred on morally developing human beings, a process which requires that they acquire a genuine or true human existence. The view of social transformation centred on a vision of a humane society might speak to what Stephen Bantu Biko (2004, 74) anticipated when he spoke of black cultures bestowing 'the greatest possible gift [to the world] — a more human face'. The underlying approach to development anticipated here is that development is value-and-human-centred, and it should not be reduced to technological and infrastructural advancements.[2]

Furthermore, the framework of development ethics construes development in very broad terms that encapsulate all crucial spheres of human existence — the human, social and natural. This view takes a holistic approach to development, which integrates the three facets of existence mentioned above (Nel 2008). On this ethico-conceptual framework, development is defined as a 'process of socio-economic-political change which takes place in a country (locality, region)' (Dower 2008, 184). I am aware that this definition is inadequate insofar as it only associates development with a process of social transformation, it does not yet specify the specific results that characterises such a process. I submit that the specific normative content of such social transformations will be specified when we articulate an African theory of development. I will say more on development ethics and its conception of development below.

I structure this chapter as follows. I begin by discussing the framework of development ethics. This will provide us with a model to think about an African conception of development. In the second section I rehearse the dual nature of the ethics of personhood — moral perfection and moral status. In the third section, I respond to the three questions posed by development ethics in the light of personhood, namely: (1) what is a good life? (2) what is a just society? and (3) how ought we to relate to nature (environment)? In the final section, I consider what personhood proffers in terms of the ethics of means.

Development ethics as a framework for thinking about development

In one of his essays providing a rough history of development, Ben Fine (2009) mentions attempts to construct or articulate conceptions of development with a *human face*. Specifically, he mentions the efforts of academics such as Amartya Sen (2001) and his capabilities approach. This approach embodies a hope that the discourse of development can be saved from the clutches of economics and become part of a robust social science discourse. It is indicative of a new approach to the study of development, called *development ethics*. This relatively new field of inquiry understands development as a 'philosophical' and 'ethical' enterprise (Goulet 1996, 5; Crocker 1991, 458). At the heart of development ethics is a conception of development underpinned by three philosophical questions (Goulet 1996). The first question pertains to the nature of a *good* life — what is a good life? The second one grapples with specifying the nature of a *just* society — what is a just society? The last one involves considering our relationship and duties to the environment — we have duties to some facets of the environment? (Goulet 1996). In other words, development ethics rethinks the concept of development in the light of answering the above-mentioned value-laden philosophical questions.

In terms of this new field of inquiry, we should understand development primarily in ethical (rather than strictly in economic) terms (Sen 1987, 2–3; Goulet 1996, 1). The point is not so much to dismiss economics in the discourse of development, but rather to correctly understand its role as a *means* and to understand development as a moral enterprise pivoting on ultimate moral values such as freedom or wellbeing (Sen 1987; Kudadjie 1992). Ultimately, we are to understand development as a process of socio-political and economic change from one state to another underpinned by particular moral ends, like wellbeing (Dower 2008, 184). The desired state is one that is characterised as an *improvement*, as *desirable* or *good* — all value laden terms (Keita 2004). In other words, talk of development involves the recognition of some ultimate *moral* end(s), be they wellbeing, dignity or *eudaimonia* (Goulet 1996). In fact, Goulet, one of the pioneers of development ethics, states that –

> Ethical judgements regarding the good life, the just society, and the *quality* of relations among people and with nature always serve, explicitly or implicitly, as operational criteria for development planners and researchers. *Development ethics is that new discipline which deals* ex professo *with such normative issues.* (1996, 2; emphasis mine)

Thus, we appreciate the fact that talk of development essentially involves moral goals understood in three spheres of human existence, namely: the personal sphere (concerning the good, be it characterised as wellbeing or dignity); the socio-economic sphere (concerning a good or just society) and the environmental sphere (to which facets of nature do we owe moral duties? Alternatively, what reasons ground our duties to protect the environment?)

Development ethics is not only concerned with questions of (moral) ends; it is *equa*lly concerned with questions of means — the ethics of means (Dower 2008). The ethics of means is crucial insofar as it serves as a necessary intervention in the process of development, given that there are many ways to go about pursuing this end. The ethics of means intervenes by providing a moral-theoretical decision-making procedure for selecting routes to development that are morally correct. In this light, development ethics imagines development entirely as a moral concept insofar as both the means (*qua* options for pursuing it) and ends it prescribes (*qua* the very goal(s) of development, like wellbeing) are intrinsically moral.

I believe that this rough picture of development ethics already begins to suggest why it is hasty to jettison the discourse on development from African moral-political conversations. This approach to development is robust for several reasons. Firstly, it is culture- and region-sensitive. In other words, it allows various cultures and regions to draw from their own axiological resources to reflect on the kind of socio-political change they want to see (Crocker 1991). This is important insofar as it is (1) consistent with the ideals of the independence of Africans and their cultures (Wiredu 1980); (2) one way to challenge imperialism, hegemony and neo-colonialism in the discourse of development (Dei 2000; Keita 2004); and (3) an African perspective, which will be important for a cross-cultural dialogue in our quest for global ethics (Dower 2008). Secondly, it offers a broad concept of development that covers the social, political, economic and environmental dimensions of human and non-human existence, which makes it consistent with calls for sustainable development and the United Nations Development Programmes goal and standards of achievement

(Hopkins 1991; Anand and Sen 1994; Loewe 2012). It is in this light that I will be using this conceptual framework to pursue an African perspective of development.[3]

To the best of my knowledge, there has been no attempt in the literature to construe an African conception of development *qua* personhood in the light of the paradigm of development ethics.[4] If development ethics seeks to give an account of development that is philosophically and contextually sensitive, then it strikes me as a worthwhile framework to adopt. My preoccupation, in this chapter, will be on giving an account of a just society.[5] That is, I set myself the goal of answering the three philosophical questions posed by development ethics, drawing from the moral insights provided by the concept of personhood. To offer philosophical responses to these questions in the light of personhood amounts to proffering an African conception of a good life, a just socio-political order and environmental ethics. Furthermore, for this personhood-based conception of development to be complete, it must also furnish us with a moral-theoretical *corpus* regarding the means it prescribes for pursuing development (the ethics of means); that is, the principle it will prescribe for selecting among competing options for pursuing the goal of development.

Three questions of development ethics in the light of personhood

Personhood and the good human life

Here, I briefly rehearse an account of a good life according to the discourse of personhood (see Chapters 2 and 3). The discourse on development ethics accounts for development in terms of a basic, or final, moral value. To have an account of a good life involves knowing the final good prescribed by the idea of personhood, which will serve as the goal of development. The idea of the 'good' life should be understood as a strict moral issue, which involves norms and values that define what we consider the essence of morality. In the book, I have been arguing that the idea of personhood is a doubled-edged sword. On the one hand, it embodies a perfectionist, or self-realisation, approach to morality; on the other, it embodies an ethics of dignity that captures it in terms of the capacity for sympathy. Below, to elaborate on the view of the good according to personhood, I remind the reader of the perfectionist or self-realisation approach.

The goal of morality, in the self-realisation approach, is for the moral agent to realise the potential of her human nature, which scholars of African thought usually explain in terms of moral practice or virtue. Menkiti expresses this moral vision in this fashion –

> The African emphasised the rituals of incorporation and the overarching necessity of learning the social rules by which the community lives, so that what was initially biologically given can come to attain social selfhood, i.e., become a person with all the inbuilt excellencies implied by the term. (Menkiti 1984, 173)

Note that Mogobe Ramose — one of the leading scholars of ubuntu/personhood — also thinks of it as a self-realisation ethic, characterising the moral goal thus –

> To be a human being is to affirm one's humanity by recognising the humanity of others and, on that basis, establish humane relations with them…One is enjoined, yes, commanded as it were, to actually become a human being. (1999, 52)

Another influential scholar of ubuntu/personhood, former Justice Yvonne Mokgoro, makes the following comment regarding the maxim 'a person is a person through other persons' — it 'implies that during one's lifetime, one is constantly challenged by others, practically, to achieve self-fulfilment through a set of collective social ideals.' Mothlabi and Munyaka (2009, 65) inform us that 'it is more accurate to say that Ubuntu is a person's self-realization…'

The logic of a perfectionist or self-realisation approach to ethics makes the focus and goal of morality human nature, or at least some facet of it. In this moral view, human nature is conceived as having the potential to transition from mere biology to a bearer of moral norms or virtue (Menkiti 2004; Ikuenobe 2016). Hence, in this view, the good life is a function entirely of the perfection of the character of the individual. The expectation is that the moral agent's character will be virtuous insofar as it manifests love, forgiveness, friendliness, generosity and so on. To judge some agent to be a person amounts to viewing her as leading a morally flourishing life insofar as her life exudes virtues that connect her with the community (see Wiredu 2009).

The other facet of the ethics of personhood embodies a theory of dignity. I remind the reader of the following considerations. Remember that the idea of personhood embodies a dual approach towards thinking about the good. Above, we just considered the character-centred facet of personhood as a moral theory, where the agent's chief moral responsibility is the acquisition or development of moral excellence (perfection). The moral perfection part of this moral view focuses on agency. It is therefore called the agent-centred notion of personhood. Furthermore, it focuses on how the agent actualises her agency to pursue a virtuous character (Behrens 2013; Molefe 2019a).

This facet of the ethics of personhood focuses on the moral patient; it specifies which beings count as morally valuable in the natural world. For some entity to count as a bearer of superlative value, that is, to be a possessor of dignity, the entity ought to possess the capacity to pursue personhood. In the previous chapters, I explained the capacity to pursue *virtue* in terms of sympathy. Hence, the good life, according to the idea of personhood, is constituted by the capacity to pursue a morally virtuous life (dignity), which engenders duties of respect for moral agents (recognition respect) towards it. Those entities that go on to develop these capacities and end up leading morally virtuous lives, deserve appraisal respect.

Put simply, the good life revolves around how agents (and their societies) treat their capacities for virtue. Those that develop and perfect these capacities will be living a good moral life, and those that do not will be living below what is expected and possible for human existence. In this moral view, the good revolves around capacities for human excellence and the possibilities for achieving it. Below, I consider a conception of a just society in the light of personhood.

Personhood and a just society

To begin our explication of a just society in the light of personhood, we need to be clear regarding what it prescribes as the good. Above, we captured the good *qua* personhood in two related ways. In the first instance, we pointed out that the good is a function of leading a morally virtuous life. In the second, we highlighted the fact that the good is a function of the capacity to pursue a good life. The good is captured in terms of the capacity of the individual to pursue personhood. As the first approximation of a conception of a good society, I postulate that it is one that allows human beings to pursue moral perfection — moral virtue. I imagine that a just society, according to personhood, is one that maximises opportunities and conditions for human beings to be able to realise themselves. An unjust society, then, is one that cripples its members by reducing opportunities for them to be able to lead true human lives.

Lansana Keita captures the suggestion of a just society in this fashion –

> To answer the question concerning the political life and structures of an advanced Africa, I begin by posing a thought experiment question. The question is: If one were about to be born but without knowledge as to one's prospective economic and sociological status, gender, talents, health, family, and so on, into what kind of society would one wish to arrive? *The answer is that any individual would hope to enter a society in which he or she would be guaranteed economic security for survival purposes, optimal conditions for self-development and self-realisation and maximal conditions for freedom and self-expression.* In other words, the individual about to enter human society would necessarily hope to enter a society that is structured in such way that human welfare in all its dimensions would be maximised… (2004, 124; emphasis mine)

Above, Keita gives us a picture of a just social structure. In his view, a just socio-economic order is one that provides optimal conditions for personal development or self-realisation. Put in the light of the idea of personhood, a just society is not one that has many of its people actually leading morally virtuous lives. The essence of it is characterised by the provisions of at least basic conditions required for the pursuit of personhood to be possible. An unjust social order will characteristically create obstacles to such a pursuit. For example, the colonisation of African societies; the slavery of African people in many parts of the world (particularly in the Americas and Europe); and apartheid in South Africa, are good examples of unjust socio-political orders. Under conditions such as colonisation, slavery, economic exploitation and exclusion, and 'apartheid' in America and South Africa, the possibility of pursuing personhood is rendered almost impossible. One's capacity to realise a true human life, characterised by moral excellence, is, in such conditions, in jeopardy.

In precise terms, the unjust nature of these socio-political and economic arrangements is characterised by the violation of what is most precious about being human — the capacity for sympathy. An unjust social order undermines the very essence of being human — the capacity for virtue [sympathy]. This capacity is necessary for the possibility of personhood. We may call this the *dignity condition* of justice. The most important moral-political feature of a just social order *qua* personhood revolves around recognising the humanity of others. On this understanding of personhood, a just society is one that recognises the humanity of others for what it is (the capacity for virtue) and the possibilities enfolded in it. It is for this reason that Ramose notes –

> Most African languages have in their vernacular a saying synonymous with the Sotho, *motho ke motho ka batho*. This means that to be human is to affirm one's humanness by recognising the same *quality* in others and, on that basis, establishing humane relations with them. (2009, 308; emphasis mine)

Here, Ramose informs us that the discourse on personhood (ubuntu) requires us to recognise the *quality* that embodies the moral preciousness of others' humanity. It is safe to assume that this *quality* is the same among all human beings, all things being equal. Personhood, primarily, requires us to recognise the *quality* that is a feature of all human beings as the basis for a proper moral-political response towards them. The discourse on personhood, therefore, requires us to have a correct understanding of human beings and the *quality* that marks them out as special in the moral world, or what makes them count as a 'privileged' part of nature (Ramose 2009, 309). To further make this point, Ramose (2009, 2010) quotes one of the famous sayings among some African cultures — *feta kgomo o tshware motho*. He construes this to amount to the following –

> …the practice of *feta kgomo o tshware motho*…requires moral education based upon the principles of sharing, concern for one another and the subordination of wealth to the dignity of the human person as *motho*. (2010, 301)

The word *motho*, descriptively, in seSotho refers to a human being, and *kgomo* refers to a cow. Cows, in most African traditional cultures, represent wealth. The significance of this saying is that it is reminiscent of Kant's distinction between price and worth (Kant [1785] 1996). The value of a cow is captured in terms of price insofar as it varies according to the external circumstances of the culture in question. The value of a human being (motho) is captured in terms of worth insofar as it is inherent and absolute. In other words, in the discourse of personhood, we are required to recognise the *qua*lity of other human beings. This requirement is a call for us to recognise the high value of humanity (dignity). We can conclude that at the heart of the discourse on personhood *qua* a just social order is the recognition of the dignity of human beings that surpasses all other values. It is the recognition of the fact of this superlative value that impels us to react positively to others by forming sharing and caring relations with them.

One insight that emerges above is that a just social order is a function, primarily, of (1) recognising the human *qua*lity — the capacity for virtue — that embodies the inherent worth or dignity of human beings; and (2) responding to their high value by forming robust social relationships with others characterised by other-regarding duties. So, at the heart of the discourse on personhood is the creation of a society that is responsive to the dignity of all human beings. Recognising others' humanity throws us into particular kinds of social relations with them, where we share and care for them (Ramose 2009, 302). At this point, one may inquire why the idea of dignity is fundamental in accounting for a just social order.

The idea of dignity is crucial to capture the essence of a just social order for two reasons. Firstly, one of the plausible features of the idea of dignity is that it embodies an egalitarian approach to a socio-political and economic life. The idea of dignity imagines *equa*l respect towards all human beings merely because they possess the relevant capacity for virtue. The mere possession of this capacity is the sole ground that captures the *equa*lity of all human beings. Some individuals might have more of this capacity than others, but that consideration is largely beside the point. The point is that anyone with a minimum threshold of the relevant capacity has *equa*l dignity. This point is crucial because dignity is not a function of the *use* of the relevant ontological feature; it is a function merely of possessing it. Hence, every individual with the capacity for virtue is owed *equa*l moral consideration by the state and society.

The idea of dignity, in its egalitarian posture, is politically powerful since it forbids attempts to dehumanise others on arbitrary grounds. Manifestations of racism and racist social orders, or patriarchy and a sexist social order, ought to be repudiated since they fail to treat individuals equally as they do no recognise their capacity for virtue. All moral patients, without regard to their sex, race, education, culture, class, etc., that have dignity *qua* the capacity for virtue deserve e*qua*l recognition in the moral-political community.

The second reason the idea of dignity is crucial for a just social order is that it provides crucial moral-political protections. In other words, the idea of dignity serves as a *constraint* or agent-centred restriction (McNaughton and Rawling 2006). This implies that in the pursuit of the good we may not violate human dignity or harm human beings (Hurley 1995; Toscano 2011). These socio-political protections associated with the idea of dignity make it suitable to protect the lives of individuals against powerful institutions and individuals. Practically, the state cannot instrumentalise individuals (that is, treat them as mere means). It cannot, for example, attempt to build social trust among its citizens by framing an individual for a crime she did not commit, for the sake of the greater good (Donnelly 2009).

These two considerations related to the idea of dignity — (1) its e*qua*lising function and (2) its function as a constraint — render it suitable to ground a plausible account of a just society. Dignity recognises the e*qua*lity of all human beings and it offers all of them social protections against arbitrary and unnecessary harms. This part of justice, which emphasises e*qua*lity of moral patients and their political protections, can largely be understood as capturing the universal negative duties that the state and individuals in the society owe to moral patients. It specifies dignity as the ground for such duties (Toscano, 2011).[6]

We are yet to comment on the place and relevance of positive duties in this moral-political view of a good society. The primary condition of a just social order is the recognition of the capacity for sympathy in virtue of which human beings are intrinsically valuable. The reader would do well to remember that, above, we noted that it is not enough merely to recognise the human *qua*lity that affords us dignity (i.e. to recognise a negative duty to constrain our conduct towards beings of dignity). We should also marry this recognition of the dignity of individuals which they have in virtue of possessing the capacity for sympathy to positive duties. The idea that we must respond positively to beings of dignity entails the view that such beings attract general, positive duties (Loschke 2017; Jaworska and Tannenbaum 2018). I must emphasise that the duties imagined here are both negative and positive in nature, with the African perspective placing more value on positive duties than one tends to find in the Western tradition. The reason for this is that negative duties are generally easy to execute since they only require that we mind our own business and not interfere with the lives of others, which is generally explained by appeal to the idea of negative liberty (Berlin 1958; Gyekye 2004).

The discourse on general duties, particularly positive duties, associated with the idea of personhood is captured in the literature in terms of the idea of the *common good* (see Gyekye 1992; Wiredu 1992; Eze 2009; Molefe 2017b, 2018, 2019a). The logic here is that when we have recognised what it means to be human in terms of our capacity for virtue/sympathy, it is crucial that we (the state, its institutions, communities, families and individuals) supply the goods necessary for individuals to be able to pursue personhood. The 'common good' refers to the basic goods (be they social, political or economic) that are necessary for a human being to pursue moral perfection (Wiredu 1992; Gyekye 1992, 2004; Wall 2012). In the African moral-political literature, the idea of the common good is usually captured by appeal to the Siamese crocodile with two heads and one stomach. Gyekye comments thus on this moral imagery –

> The part of the motif relevant to moral thought is the single stomach…The common stomach…*indicates that at least the basic interests of all the members of the community are identical*. It can therefore be interpreted to be symbolizing… the good of all the individuals within a society. (2010, n.p.)

The idea of the common good is predicated on the view that human beings are identical at least when it comes to possessing that ontological feature of human nature that makes the pursuit of personhood possible. This view imagines a basket of needs — a single stomach — necessary for the moral life (Gyekye 2004). In other words, the idea of the common good refers to the trans-cultural basic goods that each human individual requires to be able to pursue a moral life. The absence of these would lead to handicapped or unfortunate lives (Gyekye 2004).

It is for this reason that in another place Gyekye (1997, 67; emphasis mine) refers to these basic and commonly shared goods as '*human* goods'. These basic human goods cover a 'list of objective goods' necessary for human perfection (Wall 2012). The list covers all areas of human life — the political institutions and other social facets that make properly human life possible. It is for this reason that Gyekye notes –

> The pursuit of the good of *all* is the goal of the communitarian society, which the African society is. A sense of the common good — *which is a core of shared values* — is the underlying presupposition of African social morality. (2010, n.p.; emphasis mine)

The basic assumption of the discourse of personhood is that there are many areas in which human beings manifest diversity and divergence, particularly in the domain of culture as regarding song and dance, greetings, styles of dress and so on (Wiredu 1980). However, when it comes to what a human being requires in order to transition from merely being human to becoming a person (a moral saint), there is a core of shared basic goods that she must have access to (Gyekye 2004, 2010). Thus, to talk of the common good is to talk of the core goods all human beings need in order to realise themselves.

In the light of the above, we observe that a just society is one that recognises and respects each individual as a being of intrinsic worth and responds to this fact by ensuring the availability of the basic basket of goods for the individual to be able to pursue moral perfection. An unjust society is one that does not recognise what it means to be a human and does not provide these goods.

Note that having the status of dignity secures the requirement for all moral patients to be accorded *equa*l respect and provides protection against unwarranted and unjustified harms from the state, society or individuals. The provision of the common good makes it possible for individuals to live a dignified life. The crucial point to notice here is that, it is one thing for human beings, as a matter of fact, to have dignity since they possess the relevant capacities; but, it is quite another for them to be dignified, which is a function of two considerations. Firstly, it is a function of the provision of the common goods. Without the provision of the common goods, the individual will not be able to pursue a life of virtue. Such an existence is not dignifying. Secondly, the individual has a duty to use the common good — by exercising her agency — to achieve a dignified life.

We have now drawn a three-part distinction related to dignity in accounting for a just society. Firstly, we noted that by merely possessing the relevant capacities, the individual has the status of dignity *equa*l to that of every other human being. Secondly, we pointed to the provision of the common good as dignifying. Here, the provision of the common good is dignifying insofar as it provides conditions for a dignified existence, where the individual has access to basic amenities in order to be able to lead a decent human life — such as shelter, healthy food, education, access to healthcare, stable political conditions and so on (Gyekye 2010). Thirdly, we said that a dignified life emerges as a result of the agent exercising her natural capacities, through her agency, and in the light of enabling conditions (*qua* the common good) to achieve personhood.

To offer concreteness to this talk of a just society as imagined through the prism of personhood, I reflect that it explains why colonisation and apartheid were moral-political evils. Firstly, colonisation and apartheid were evil precisely because they failed to recognise the dignity of the African peoples. Failure to recognise the humanity of African people is tantamount to their dehumanisation (Biko [1978] 2004). This dehumanisation was actualised by putting in place socio-political structures that systematically removed the basic goods that people required to lead a human life. In other words, these political systems were unjust because they locked Africans into an 'amoral' situation by refusing to recognise their capacity for virtue. The systems treated Africans as beings without moral ends (Molefe 2018). To be put into this 'amoral' situation is tantamount to being arbitrarily removed from the moral community, and thus being reduced to a status of a *thing* (Molefe and Magam 2019).

The dispossession of African people's land, the destruction of their history, culture and heritage, their economies and political structures, was precisely the political work of disrupting the common good. In other words, taking away land and all the cultural inventions available for imagining and navigating life subjected African peoples to a life of indignity, which degraded and denied them an opportunity to exercise and develop their humanity. The political system of apartheid in South Africa, for example, systematically rendered the very possibility of personhood as the moral goal almost impossible. The important point to appreciate is that the 'amoralisation' of human beings coupled with the removal of the common good makes it impossible for human beings to pursue moral perfection. Put in precise terms, these unjust systems severed the connection between the humanity of Africans and the possibility of morality. The defining feature of a just society revolves around enhancing the connection between human beings (with the capacity to pursue virtue) and the creation of conditions where possibilities for pursuing a dignified life (achieving personhood) are open and available to all.

Another way to illuminate these two crucial conditions for a just social order is by revisiting the Marikana massacre. In the Marikana massacre, police shot and killed at least 38 miners in South Africa (see Metz 2016; Molefe and Magam 2019). Marikana poses as an interesting moral-political site for philosophical scrutiny in post-colonial, post-apartheid South Africa, especially in the light of personhood as a theory of just social order. Before the police shot the miners, they were engaged in an illegal strike demanding a wage increase. Places like Marikana in post-apartheid South Africa, and many mining areas in Africa, are a testament to the continued reality of cheap black labour. Cheap, or free, black labour was a central facet of colonial and apartheid capitalism in South Africa (Biko [1978] 2004).

The major weakness of the post-apartheid state revolves around its failure to redress some of these historical injustices. Post-apartheid South Africa cannot be just or sever its link to an evil history of exploitative and racial capitalism if it does not aim to eradicate the injustices of the past, like cheap black labour. The state in South Africa *qua* the African National Congress responded to the Marikana massacre by recommending a commission of inquiry. The problem began, in my view, when the state specified the terms of reference of the commission of inquiry; it never sought to properly situate and understand the cause of the strike in its overall context of cheap black labour that began with the discovery of diamonds in Kimberley in 1862 and gold in 1886 on the Witwatersrand.

Recently, Thaddeus Metz offered a moral-political evaluation of the response of the state to the Marikana massacre (Metz 2016). In his view, the discourse of personhood (ubuntu) would have proposed, as the moral-political response to the Marikana massacre, not a commission of inquiry, but something like the Truth and

Reconciliation Commission, and consequently, the response of a state that highly prized ubuntu (personhood) ought to have been the prescription of *reconciliation* as the best solution.

It is important to notice that Metz, in his analysis of the Marikana situation, says nothing about the role and responsibilities of the private firm against which the miners were striking. He does not offer a critical scrutiny of capitalism and its complicity in apartheid and post-apartheid South Africa, particularly in creating indecent lives by way of offering extremely low salaries to black miners. Metz does not make any suggestions or comments about the core issue from the perspective of the miners — the question of decent working conditions and a reasonable salary. The root problem signalled by a three-month-long unprotected strike — cheap black labour — is not given any attention at all. This root problem has been a persisting feature of mines even in the 'new' South Africa. By ignoring the intersecting issues of racial capitalism, cheap labour, weak government and so on, Metz unwittingly invokes the ethical, in the form of personhood (ubuntu) *qua* reconciliation, to maintain the status *quo* of economic oppression, exploitation and exclusion. This way of conceiving of just societies, by only emphasising reconciliation, through the invocation of personhood [ubuntu], is bound to fail.

I think reconciliation in and of itself is important in the attempt to resolve the history of conflict and division in a society. It is crucial to appreciate, however, that reconciliation, by itself, is not sufficient as a moral-political solution. More is urgently required in imagining a robust, just society. The state has a duty to create moral-political conditions that affirm the humanity (dignity) of all, particularly of victims. This affirmation revolves around recognising the fact that victims, and others, are beings of dignity, and, given this status, deserve utmost moral regard. We further need to respond by providing the basic means and resources necessary for a dignified existence. I believe that Leonhard Praeg's analysis of post-apartheid South Africa endorses the importance of the common good in responding to past injustices in the quest of pursuing a just social order –

> Is it not untimely to invoke notions of our shared humanity (brotherhood of former enemies) as long as we live in *a society where there is no real sharing of real resources*. At what point does the demand to honor the spirit of ubuntu turn into an instrument of oppression, rather than a liberating act of humanism, because it has been used to maintain the status quo? Should all talk of ubuntu not be temporarily suspended in order to create the necessary space for the agitation of political and economic conditions that, while temporarily at odds with ubuntu style notions of brotherhood, will nonetheless *create the necessary economic conditions for bringing about the truly ethical*, a world of true ubuntu in which we can meaningfully substantiate talk of shared humanity with the fact of a more equitable sharing of resources? (2014, 18; emphasis mine)

In this analysis, I read Praeg to be complaining about how the discourse on ubuntu is usually invoked in ways that problematise the legacy of colonisation and apartheid in the so-called new South Africa. The discourse of virtue, brotherhood and/or sisterhood and compassion, usually associated with personhood, has been used to sanitise present and past oppressions. The prevalent discourse on personhood refuses to appreciate that its radical facets demand substantive socio-political changes, which ought to be attended by the provision of the real material and political goods that will bring about the truly ethical — the creation of a social space where individuals can pursue moral perfection and enjoy true brotherhood (reconciliation).

In this light, we cannot talk of healing and redeeming our society until we are serious about addressing the conditions that cause the moral injury of African people.[7] The idea of 'moral injury', in the feminist discourse, refers to 'the shattering of trust that compromises our ability to love' (Gilligan 2014, 90). We cannot meaningfully speak of *brotherhood* of all humanity or *shared humanity*, as imagined by personhood, if we are not *equally* committed to bringing about the conditions where human beings are equitably exposed to real resources to realise themselves — to build their self-esteem, self-worth, and trust towards society, government and former oppressors. Thus, the idea of personhood is a critical moral discourse that challenges us to rethink a just society by characterising all human beings as the focus of a politics of *equal* moral regard. The idea also requires the provision of necessities for human beings to flourish. Without these, discourse of brotherhood and shared humanity is a sham. The truly ethical, as imagined in the discourse of personhood, requires the creation of dignifying conditions, which are characterised by maximal opportunities for individuals to realise themselves. It is only in contexts where individuals are empowered to be human again that we can rightly speak of reconciliation.

So, a just society is one that recognises the dignity of individuals and provides basic goods that enable individuals to live dignified lives. This analysis has given us an opportunity to reflect on past and present injustices. Now, I move on to consider the question of personhood and the environment.

Personhood and the environment

Another important question related to development in the framework of development ethics revolves around our relationship and duties towards the environment. The reader will remember (from Chapter 4) that the idea of personhood embodies a weak version of anthropocentrism. The defining feature of weak anthropocentrism is that it accords a higher moral status to human beings and a partial one to non-human animals. In this view, it would be immoral, all things being *equal*, to kill non-human animals for sport or food, when there is no scarcity of food. A robust environmental ethics, however, goes beyond animals to encompass rivers, lakes, mountains, forests and so on (Brennan and Lo 2016). The crucial question to consider is whether the idea of personhood imposes duties on us as moral agents towards the environment in general.

The idea of personhood does not accord any intrinsic value to most parts of the environment like trees, mountains and so on in their own right. The reason for this is that these do not have the capacity for sympathy. Alternatively, we deny them moral status because they cannot be affected by the lack or presence of sympathy. For one to be receptive to sympathy, at the very least, one should be conscious and sentient or be the subject of a life. Since much of the environment does not count as either a subject or an object of sympathy, it does not have moral status. In this light, we can conclude that we do not have any direct moral duties towards the broader environment.

The fact that most parts of the environment have no moral status at all implies that the environment in its own right does not occasion any moral concerns and duties for moral agents. This implies that we may do as we please towards it without meaningfully speaking of *harm* since we will not be dealing with moral patients. This fact regarding the environment and its lack of moral status, however, does not preclude a prudential approach towards how we relate to it. We may take ourselves to have strong *indirect* duties to protect the environment. The protection can take the form of what the literature dubs *enlightened anthropocentrism* (Keurlatz 2012; Brennan and Lo 2016). The essence of this view is that we need to take care of the environment for the sake of human beings, for current and future generations. The prudence of doing so could just be the fact that we need to live our human lives on this planet. The consequence, therefore, of harming the planet might be counterproductive insofar as it might ultimately threaten human life. For the good of human and non-human animals, we must consider ourselves to have strong indirect duties to take care of the environment as a whole. Failure to respond decisively on the issue of climate change might amount to self-sabotage insofar we will be undermining the prospect of human and non-human survival.

Above, we discussed development in the light of personhood through three ancient philosophical questions. We noted that personhood accounts for the good in terms of the capacity for virtue, which explains why we expect individuals to pursue moral perfection. With regards to a just social order, we said that it hinges primarily on the recognition of the status of the dignity of human beings and the creation of dignifying conditions of existence, which are decisive for the possibility of moral perfection. Concerning the environment, we noted that we have duties to human beings and animals, albeit that the duties to the latter are weaker since animals only have partial moral status. Concerning the environment (forests, rivers, lakes and so on), we noted that we have indirect duties towards them, which we explained by appeal to enlightened anthropocentrism.

Now let us turn the conversation to what the ethics of means entails.

Personhood and the ethics of means

Development, in the framework of development ethics, focuses on moral ends and on moral means. The end (goal) of development through the lens of personhood is the attaining of moral perfection, or at least the creation of conditions for such moral possibilities. Development ethics also requires us to focus on the 'means of means' (Dower 2008, 189–190). This concerns ethical reflections on the 'how' part of pursuing the good life and a just society. For example, Goulet's (1996) distinction between the *ethical* and *engineering* approaches to development signals the crucial difference between moral ends and means. Development as an ethical enterprise involves some basic value, which in the light of personhood is the capacity to realise oneself. Talk of economics, as an engineering approach, refers to economic growth as a *means* to development, and not as its defining essence. The means of pursuing development in terms of the provision of basic goods, be they food or infrastructure, etc., must be subjected to ethical scrutiny. This is because one can imagine firms in an economy that are corrupt in their dealings in ways that end up undermining human capacities for self-realisation. One can also imagine firms that undermine people's ways of life and cultures or ones that offer forms of employment that are precarious, dangerous, unfulfilling and generally exploitative. Take, for example, Dower's talk of means –

> One of the things which the ethics of the means brings out is the fact that development ethics has, so to speak, a number of dimensions. Much of development ethics is part of social, political or public ethics; that is, the ethical issues are about how public policies and laws can, for instance, deliver the moral goals of social justice, protect human rights, express democracy, protect the environment, or provide the right education for the next generation. (2008, 189)

My intention here is to offer a theoretical principle that will account for how the ethics of means is to be understood in the light of personhood. At the heart of the discourse of personhood is the moral goal of achieving a good character, but the moral agent can only achieve moral perfection by participating in robust social relationships. In other words, at the heart of the ethics of personhood is the importance of social relationships as the best instruments to achieve moral perfection. Godfrey Onah, cited by Metz, comments in this fashion –

> At the centre of traditional African morality is human life. Africans have a sacred reverence for life…To protect and nurture their lives, all human beings are inserted within a given community…The promotion of life is therefore the determinant principle of African traditional morality and this promotion is guaranteed only in the community. Living harmoniously within a community is therefore a moral obligation ordained by God for the promotion of life. (Metz 2007, 329)

Here, Onah offers a different moral end as the goal of African ethics — life (or vitality). My interest is the means he prescribes for securing the moral end; Onah prescribes social relationships as the best instrumental good for pursuing human flourishing. Morality, Onah informs us, is guaranteed only in the community. Further, Onah specifies that the ideal context for flourishing morally is 'living harmoniously' with others. He informs us that living harmoniously is an obligation required for achieving the moral end of promoting life (or, in our case, moral perfection). In this ethical system, human beings can only achieve the ideals of personhood by living harmoniously with others. The point here is that moral perfection is only possible in cooperative relationships. This same point is appositely captured by Munyaka and Mothlabi (2009, 71; see also pages 68, 69 and 70), thus –

> It is in the community that the individual is able to realise himself or herself as a person. The personal growth of individuals happens in community. *Only* through the cooperation, influence and contribution of others, can one understand and bring to fulfilment one's own personality.

It is also captured in Shutte's characterisation –

> The goal of morality according to this moral vision is fullness of humanity. Moral life is seen as the process of moral growth. Just as participation in community with others is the *essential means* to personal growth, so participation with others is the motive and fulfilment of the process. (2009, 96; emphasis mine)

From the above, it is clear that self-realisation is the proper moral end posited by personhood as a moral theory; and, moreover, cooperative relationships with others are thought to be the essential means for achieving such an end. The direct implication of this moral logic of means valued for pursuing development is that this ethics highly prizes paths and options that are participatory and cooperative. Development, if it is influenced by personhood, must facilitate communities of participation and cooperation, directly or by representation.

This way of thinking about means has implications for how decisions are made about which options to follow in pursuing development — consensus will be the characteristic feature of policy decision-making in the pursuit of development (Gyekye 1992; Wiredu 1996a; Matolino 2018b). In other words, policy options most consistent with personhood are those that emerge in contexts of robust deliberations that result in consensus rather than majoritarianism (Gyekye 1992). This is the case because majoritarianism marginalises the minority, whereas consensus seeks a decision that is as accommodative as possible. Under consensus there are no losers and there is no attitude of winner takes all. This is the essence of the participatory logic required by personhood (Wiredu 1996; Eze 2009).

Another crucial facet to consider in pursuing development in line with the means that prize community, is to approach it in ways that are consistent with the cultural *values* of personhood. Here, by 'values', I am specifically referring to norms that are salient and characteristic of a particular place and culture — i.e. customs (Wiredu 1992, 193; 2008, 334–336). For example, Wiredu (1980) and Metz (2007) discuss some of the dominant cultural values salient among African people: the value of consensus over majoritarianism; the fundamental goal of retribution being reconciliation and not punishment; the imagination of socially cooperative ways to build wealth/economies as opposed to individualistic and competitive ones; the distribution of goods on the moral logic of needs and care as opposed to that of rights, etc. Crucial to note is that these cultural values are consistent with a society that highly values the possibility of each individual realising her own true self. These values also emphasise the duty to respond positively to individuals that may be in need, for the sake of ensuring that they are not obstructed from the goal of their personal development.

In the light of the above, we note that the discourse on personhood will prefer those developmental paths that encourage community and cooperation. One of the central tools that will be employed to establish development policies will revolve around the value and practice of consensus. As such, the top-down and expert only approach to development is not compatible with the community-oriented ethos and ethics characteristic of personhood.

Conclusion

Above, we sought to articulate an African conception of development. To do so, we invoked development ethics as a conceptual framework to offer a robust conception of development. Development ethics conceives of development as an ethical enterprise, which is constituted by answering three questions — (1) what is a good? (2) what is a just society? and (3) how ought we to relate to the nature?

The essence of development in terms of the idea of personhood is a function of creating dignifying socio-political and economic conditions, which are preconditions for moral agents to realise themselves. A developed society is one that is characterised by maximal conditions and opportunities (the common good) that enable human beings to pursue moral perfection (the good).

In terms of our duties to the environment, we noted that personhood assigns the greatest moral status to human beings, some moral status to animals and only indirect duties to facets of the environment like mountains, rivers and forests. In terms of moral means, personhood prescribes cooperation and participation as the best way to pursue development. In other words, what does not involve us and does not take our cultural modes of being in the world seriously does not count as genuine development.

Notes
1. This chapter is part of a bigger project of relying on indigenous moral resources to articulate an African conception of personhood. This chapter benefitted from some of my ideas published in several places (see Molefe 2011, 2018, 2019c; Molefe and Magam 2019). This project started in my masters dissertation where I sought to give an ubuntu-based conception of development (2011). Then I went on to refine the idea of personhood/ubuntu (2018; Molefe and Magam 2019). The distinctive feature of this chapter is its reliance on the dual features of personhood to articulate a conception of development.

2. Martin Ajei (2007, 227) criticises attempts to reduce development to econonism because this has led to epistemicide and valuecide, among others, on the African continent. If we really seek to uncover and rediscover the true human face, we need to draw from African values associated with the discourse of ubuntu/personhood. I am in full agreement with Ajei's approach to the discourse on development in the African context; I differ with him in terms of his espousing spiritual meta-ethics that accounts for development by appeal to the ontological property and value of vitality. In this view of development, the spirtual and moral property of vitality is taken to be the basis for African ethics (Ajei 2007, 196). I stipulate a naturalist meta-ethics, which I derive from the idea of personhood.

3 I admit that the framework of development ethics was born in the West. That fact, in and of itself, does not make it objectionable. I say so for two major reasons. Firstly, it is user-friendly to advance an African agenda as it explicitly allows differing regions and cultures to answer the three crucial questions that embody the idea and ideal of development drawing from their own cultural resources. Secondly, the three questions that constitute the idea of development regarding the good life, a just society and our relation to the environment strike me as universal ones. Every culture and people has to reflect on these philosophical questions. The fact that the idea of development ethics is understood in primarily ethical terms means that it is open to criticisms and amendments guided by plausible moral intuitions and views. Hence, I find it plausible and useful to articulate an African perspective of development.

4 I am aware that John Klaasen (2017) attempts to articulate a personhood-based conception of development. He draws his notion of personhood from influential scholars of African moral thought like Menkiti, Gyekye and Tutu. In principle, I agree with Klaasen that the idea of personhood can contribute to the discourse on development. The major difference between the view presented in this chapter and Klaasen's is in two areas. Firstly, Klaasen is not clear regarding how he understands the idea of personhood. He appears to conflate the cultural and moral concepts of personhood. For my part, I limit myself to the moral notions of personhood *qua* moral status (explained in terms of the capacity for sympathy) and moral perfection (which manifests through a virtue laden disposition and deportment). Secondly, it is not entirely clear what Klaasen has in mind when he talks of 'development'. He seems to associate it with personal responsibility. Personal responsibility is undoubtedly one part of development, but this misses the crucial questions regarding the structural features of society and the conditions and opportunities required as pre-

conditions for it (personal responsibility) to be meaningful. Hence, I employ development ethics as a conceptual framework to articulate a robust conception of development, which accommodates personal responsibility *qua* the pursuit of moral perfection (the good), structural issues (just society) and the environment in which we live our lives.

5   The reader will do well to remember that in Chapters 2, 3 and 4, I have already extensively reflected on the question of the good [life] and our duties to the environment. It is for this reason that I devote more attention to the issue of a good or just society in this chapter.

6   This is not to suggest that the idea of dignity does not secure positive duties. In fact, talk of dignity does entail positive duties for moral agents. All things being e*qua*l, moral agents have strong duties to aid beings of dignity. The reader should notice that in the Western tradition, the negative duties embodied in the constraints associated with dignity are almost absolute — they are *stringent* requirements; and the duties to aid are *strong*, and not stringent (Jaworska and Tannenbaum 2018). In the African tradition, the duty to aid, associated with dignity, is as stringent as the constraints. This stringency is captured in terms of the idea of the common good.

7   In the main, I use the word 'African' in South Africa in broad terms that include all groups that were oppressed by apartheid — coloureds, Indians and black people. I am aware that, in some sense, one can argue that white women were also 'oppressed' in that patriarchy prevailed in this social group and many women were economically excluded. My focus, however, is on black, coloured and Indian people.

Conclusion

One way to understand this book is as a tribute to Ifeanyi Menkiti, who passed away recently.[2] Menkiti was the first to bring the idea of personhood, which is the focus of this book, to our philosophical attention. The Department of Philosophy at the University of Johannesburg organised a tribute for Menkiti. Thaddeus Metz, Edwin Etieyibo, Anthony Oyowe, leading scholars of Menkiti's moral-political philosophy, a few postgraduate students and I were invited to participate in this event. All presentations, in my opinion, were of great philosophical value and revealed much about Menkiti as a person (human being) and philosopher. The presentation by Metz in particular caught my attention because it raised some of the weaknesses he believes are inherent in Menkiti's moral-political philosophy of personhood, which I hope this book adequately addresses.

In his philosophical exposition and evaluation of Menkiti's moral-political philosophy, Metz raised two specific objections. Firstly, he argued that Menkiti's idea of personhood does not have resources to secure the individualistic facets that ought to be a feature of a robust human life. The major concern seems to be that the idea of personhood does not have a place for self-regarding considerations and duties. Related to this is the concern that revolves around the view that personhood cannot account for individual uniqueness (see Tshivhase, 2013). Secondly, Metz observed that Menkiti's moral view of personhood seems to be anthropocentric in a way that is objectionable. This concern ought to be taken seriously, particularly if we are moved by the moral intuition that speciesism is morally objectionable as are racism and sexism. In this light, a plausible concept and conception of personhood ought to embody a robust animal ethics. In Metz's view, as things stand, Menkiti's view fails the test of embodying a plausible moral view that eschews speciesism.

I also noted in this book that Oyowe raises trenchant criticisms of the idea of personhood, specifically those of Menkiti. Two such criticisms stand out for me. In the first place, he argues that the idea of personhood fails to cohere with our modern moral-political intuitions that espouse egalitarianism as a feature of a robust society (see Oyowe 2018). The source of this concern is that the agent-centred notion of personhood, what he refers to as the strongly normative view of personhood, is inegalitarian as it distributes respect relative to moral conduct. Secondly, as we observed in Chapter 3, Oyowe is of the view that personhood embodies a political view that inferiorises, marginalises and secondarises women in society. As before, Oyowe's criticism pivots on how the idea of personhood fails to embody an egalitarian moral view.

In this book, I have sought to offer a philosophical interpretation of personhood that explores and exposes its robustness. I do so by proposing that we appreciate the dual features of the moral view of personhood. The one facet of personhood embodies an agent-centred theory of value that accounts for morality in terms of personal perfection. The aim of morality, in this view, is for the agent to develop a virtuous character, which exudes excellences of character, like love, compassion, generosity, altruism, care, and so on. The other facet of personhood accounts for the expectation that individuals ought to pursue moral perfection by appeal to the fact that they have the capacity for virtue (sympathy), an account of dignity. In other words, the view that emerges here is that the virtue of sympathy is foundational and characterises moral excellence in African moral thought. It speaks to the fact that the basic human capacity that needs to be developed is that of sympathy.

The literature has tended to focus on the agent-centred facet of personhood. The originality of this book is its focus on the idea of dignity that is inherent in the idea of personhood. The two components of the ethics of personhood, moral perfection and dignity, I have argued, embody a robust moral view that is germane to moral theory and applied ethics, particularly those revolving around dignity and social justice. To reveal the robustness of personhood, I invoked its conception of dignity *qua* the capacity for sympathy to reflect on disparate applied ethics themes of women, animals and development.

The robustness of the idea of personhood, therefore, is revealed by its ability to respond to some of the objections raised against it. A careful analysis of the idea of personhood indicates that it is intrinsically self-regarding. That is, it makes the capacity for sympathy the focus of morality, where the agent has a duty to develop this feature. This means that the idea of personhood is individualistic since it makes the individualistic feature of the individual — her character — the very focus and goal of morality. The argument that the idea of personhood is too other-oriented is misplaced and misguided. I also suggest that the idea of personhood embodies an under-explored communitarian model of uniqueness.

To deal with objections related to the question of women and animals, I rely, primarily, on the idea of moral status or dignity associated with personhood. In this view, dignity is a function of merely possessing the capacity for sympathy. To the extent that women possess the capacity for sympathy, it follows that they have dignity and are *equa*l to any other entity that has the same property. When it comes to animals, I argued that they have moral status insofar as they are largely objects of moral status. In other words, animals, as sentient beings that can be affected by how sympathetic beings treat and relate to them, should matter for their own sake. Genuine sympathy should be extended to all sentient beings. Animals only have partial moral status because they cannot pursue personhood. Hence, I observed that the idea of personhood embodies a weakly anthropocentric view. In this view, we have some duties to non-human animals but have no direct duties to the rest of the environment, like trees, mountains and so on, because they cannot be affected either positively or negatively by sympathy. I leave it to those who are committed to non-anthropocentrism to show the inadequacy of a weakly anthropocentric view and to proffer a convincing vision of their position.

In the previous chapter, I considered the question of development in African philosophy. I argued that the idea of personhood accounts for development in terms of creating a social structure that maximises conditions for possibilities for moral perfection. The society imagined here is a humane one, where each moral agent and social institution operates on the logic of sympathy that finds expression through other-regarding virtues or duties. The economy, infrastructure and technology are instruments for creating enabling conditions for securing basic goods of society for individuals to be able to morally flourish.

There are three themes that emerge in the book that will require philosophical exposition and argumentation. The common view in the literature has been that the idea of personhood is best understood in terms of virtue ethics (see Shutte 2001; Metz 2012a). One insight from the analysis that posits that sympathy is central in the discourse on personhood suggests a sentimentalist orientation. It is thus crucial that future research provides an elaborate account of sympathy in the discourse of personhood and African philosophy that will shed light on the Afro-sentimentalist view of personhood. Secondly, to account for personhood in terms of sympathy will also require some account of how emotions are understood in African thought and their relation to the idea of morality. There is little philosophical work focusing on the nature and function of emotions in African philosophy. The discourse on personhood embodies one avenue to pursue the study of emotions. Finally, future research might also want to compare the anticipated African moral sentimentalism associated personhood with the sentimentalist accounts in the Western tradition (see Slote 2010).

Bibliography

Agada, A., and Uti Ojah Egbai. 2018. "Language, Thought, and Interpersonal Communication: A Cross-Cultural Conversation on the Question of Individuality and Community." *Filosofia Theoretica* 7 (2): 141–162. doi:10.4314/ft.v7i2.9.

Ajei, M. 2007. "Africa's Development: The Imperatives of Indigenous Knowledge and Values." Doctoral thesis, University of South Africa, Pretoria.

Amin, S. 1972. "Underdevelopment and Dependence in Black Africa: Origins and Contemporary Forms." *Journal of Modern African Studies* 10 (4): 503–524. doi:10.1017/S0022278X00022801.

Anand, S., and A. Sen. 1994. *Human Development Index: Methodology and Measurement*. Human Development Report Office Occasional Papers 12. New York, NY: UNDP.

Annas, J. 1992. "Ancient Ethics and Modern Morality." *Philosophical Perspectives* 6: 119–136. doi:10.2307/2214241.

Asabere-Ameyaw, A., J. Anamuah-Mensah, G. Dei, and K. Raheem, eds. 2014. *Indigenist African Development and Related Issues: Towards a Transdisciplinary Perspective*. Rotterdam: Sense Publishers.

Beauchamp, T. 2005. "The nature of applied ethics." In *A Companion to Applied Ethics*, edited by R. G. Frey and C. H. Wellman, 1–16. Malden: Blackwell Publishing Ltd. doi:10.1002/9780470996621.ch1.

Behrens, K. 2010. "Exploring African Holism with Respect to the Environment." *Environmental Values* 19 (4): 465–484. doi:10.3197/096327110X531561.

Behrens, K. 2011. *African Philosophy, Thought and Practice and Their Contribution to Environmental Ethics*. Johannesburg: University of Johannesburg.

Behrens, K. 2013. "Two 'Normative' Conceptions of Personhood." *Quest: An African Journal of Philosophy* 25 (1-2):103–119.

Beitz, C. 2009. *The Idea of Human Rights*. Oxford: Oxford University Press. doi:10.1093/acprof:oso/9780199572458.001.0001.

Bibliography

Berlin, I. 1958. *Four Essays on Liberty*. Oxford: Oxford University Press.

Bewaji, J., and M. Ramose. 2003. "The Bewaji, Van Binsbergen and Ramose debate on 'Ubuntu'." *South African Journal of Philosophy* 22 (4): 378–415. doi:10.4314/sajpem.v22i4.31380.

Biko, S. (Original work published 1978) 2004. *I Write What I Like: a selection of his writings*. Johannesburg: Picador Africa.

Bikopo, Deogratias Biembe, and Louis-Jacques Van Bogaert. 2009. "Reflection on Euthanasia: Western and African Ntomba Perspectives on the Death of a Chief." *Developing World Bioethics* 10 (1): 42–48. doi:10.1111/j.1471-8847.2009.00255.x. PMID:19459899.

Brennan, A., and Lo, Y. 2007. "Two Conceptions of Human Dignity: Honour and Self-Determination." In *Perspectives on Human Dignity: A Conversation*, edited by J. Malpas and N. Lickiss, 43–58. Dordrecht: Springer Netherlands.

Bujo, B. 2001. *Foundations of an African Ethic: Beyond the Universal Claims of Western Morality*. New York, NY: The Crossroad Publishing Company.

Byron, M, edited by 2004. *Satisficing and Maximising: Moral Theorists on Practical Reason*. Cambridge: Cambridge University Press. doi:10.1017/CBO9780511617058.

Carter, A. 2011. "A Distinction Within Egalitarianism." *Journal of Philosophy* 108 (10): 535–554. doi:10.5840/jphil20111081029.

Chemhuru, M. 2016. *The Import of African Ontology for Environmental Ethics*. Johannesburg: University of Johannesburg.

Chemhuru, M. 2018. "African Communitarianism and Human Rights: Towards a Compatibilist View." *Theoria* 65 (157): 37–56. doi:10.3167/th.2018.6515704.

Chemhuru, M. 2018b. "Interpreting Ecofeminist Environmentalism in African Communitarian Philosophy and Ubuntu: An Alternative to Anthropocentrism." *Philosophical Papers* 48 (2): 241–264 doi:10.1080/05568641.2018.1450643..

Chimakonam, J., and V. Nweke. 2018. "Afro-Communitarianism and the Question of Rights." *Theoria* 65 (157): 78–99. doi:10.3167/th.2018.6515706.

Christman, J. 2014 [2004]. "Relational Autonomy, Liberal Individualism, and the Social Constitution of Selves." *Philosophical Studies: An International Journal for Philosophy in the Analytic Tradition* 117 (1/2): 143–164. doi:10.1023/B:PHIL.0000014532.56866.5c.

Collier, D., F. D. Hidalgo, and A. O. Maciuceanu. 2006. "Essentially contested concepts: Debates and applications." *Journal of Political Ideologies* 11 (3): 211–246. doi:10.1080/13569310600923782.

Crocker, D. 1991. "Towards Development Ethics." *World Development* 19 (5): 457–483. doi:10.1016/0305-750X(91)90188-N.

Dandala, M. 2009. "Cows Never Die: Embracing African Cosmology in the Process of Economic Growth." In *African Ethics: An Anthology of Comparative and Applied Ethics*, edited by Felix Murove, 259–277. Pietermaritzburg: UKZN Press.

Darwall, S. 1977. "Two Kinds of Respect." *Ethics* 88 (1): 36–49. doi:10.1086/292054.

Davids, I. Theron, and K. Maphunye, eds. 2009. *Participatory Development in South Africa: A Development Management Perspective*. 2nd edition. Pretoria: Van Schaik Publisher.

DeGrazia, D. 2008. "Moral Status as a Matter of Degree?" *Southern Journal of Philosophy* 46 (2): 181–98. doi:10.1111/j.2041-6962.2008.tb00075.x.

DeGrazia, D. 2013 [1993]. "Equal Consideration and Unequal Moral Status." *Southern Journal of Philosophy* 31 (1): 17–31. doi:10.1111/j.2041-6962.1993.tb00667.x.

Dei, G. 2000. "African Development: The Relevance and Implications of 'Indigenousness'." In *Indigenous Knowledges in Global Contexts: Multiple Readings of Our World*, edited by G. J. S. Dei, B. Hall, and D. Goldin-Rosenberg, 70–88. Toronto: University of Toronto Press.

Dei, G. 1993. "Sustainable development in the African context: Revisiting some theoretical and methodological issues." *Africa Development / Afrique et Developpement* 18 (2):97–110. https://www.jstor.org/stable/43657925

Deng, F. 2004. "Human Rights in the African Context." In *Companion to African Philosophy*, edited by K. Wiredu, 499–508. Oxford: Blackwell Publishing.

Donnelly, J. 1982. "Human Rights and Human Dignity: An Analytic Critique of Non-Western Conceptions of Human Rights." *American Political Science Review* 76 (2): 303-16. doi:10.1017/S0003055400187015.

Donnelly, J. 2009. *Human Dignity and Human Rights*. Denver: Josef Korbel School of International Studies.

Donnelly, J. 2015. "Normative Versus Taxonomic Humanity: Varieties of Human Dignity in the Western Tradition." *Journal of Human Rights* 14 (1): 1–22. doi:10.1080/14754835.2014.993062.

Dower, N. 2008. "The Nature and Scope of development ethics." *Journal of Global Ethics* 4 (3): 183–193. doi:10.1080/17449620802496289.

Dworkin, R. 1981a. "What is Equality? Part 1: Equality of Welfare." *Philosophy & Public Affairs* 10: 185–246.

Dworkin, R. 1981b. "What is Equality? Part 2: Equality of Resources." *Philosophy & Public Affairs* 10: 283–345.

Etieyibo, E. 2017. "Ubuntu, Cosmopolitanism and Distribution of Natural Resources." *Philosophical Papers* 46 (1): 139–162. doi:10.1080/05568641.2017.1295616.

Eze, M. 2009 [2008]. "What is African Communitarianism? Against Consensus as a Regulative Ideal." *South African Journal of Philosophy* 27 (4): 386–399. doi:10.4314/sajpem.v27i4.31526.

Eze, M. 2018. "Menkiti, Gyekye, and Beyond: Towards a Decolonisation of African Political Philosophy." *Filosofia Theoretica* 7 (2): 1–17. doi:10.4314/ft.v7i2.1.

Famanikwa, J. 2010. "How Moderate is Kwame Gyekye's Moderate Communitarianism?" *Thought and Practice: A Journal of the Philosophical Association of Kenya* 2: 65–77. doi:10.4314/tp.v2i2.64114.

Fine, B. 2009. "Development as Zombieconomics in the Age of Neoliberalism." *Third World Quarterly* 30 (5): 885–904. doi:10.1080/01436590902959073.

Formosa, P., and C. Mackenzie. 2014. "Nussbaum, Kant and the Capabilities Approach to Dignity." *Ethical Theory and Moral Practice* 17 (5): 875–892. doi:10.1007/s10677-014-9487-y.

Gilligan, C. 2013. *The Ethic of Care*. Barcelona: Fundacio Victor Grifolis.

Gilligan, C. 2014. "Moral Injury and the Ethic of Care: Reframing the Conversation about Differences." *Journal of Social Philosophy* 45 (1): 89–106. doi:10.1111/josp.12050.

Gilligan, C. 2002. "In a Different Voice." In *Ethical Theory: Classic & Contemporary Readings*, edited by L. Pojman, 682–688. London: Wadsworth Thomson Learning.

Goulet, D. 1996. [1997] "Development ethics: A New Discipline." *International Journal of Social Economics* 24 (11): 1160–1171. doi:10.1108/03068299710193543.

Gyekye, K., and K. Wiredu, eds. 1992. *Person and Community: Ghanaian Philosophical Studies, 1*. Washington, DC: Council for Research in Values and Philosophy.

Gyekye, K. 1995. *An Essay on African Philosophical Thought: The Akan Conceptual Scheme*. Philadelphia: Temple University Press.

Gyekye, K. 1997. *Tradition and Modernity: Philosophical Reflections on the African Experience*. New York: Oxford UP. doi:10.1093/acprof:oso/9780195112252.001.0001.

Gyekye, K. 2004. *Beyond Cultures: Perceiving a Common Humanity, Ghanaian Philosophical Studies*. Accra: The Ghana Academy of Arts and Sciences.

Gyekye, K. 2010. "African Ethics". *The Stanford Encyclopedia of Philosophy*, edited by E. N. Zalta. Accessed 13 October 2019. https://plato.stanford.edu/entries/african-ethics/.

Hargrove, E. 2014 [1992]. "Weak Anthropocentric Intrinsic Value." *Monist* 75 (2): 183–207. doi:10.5840/monist19927529.

Hopkins, M. 1991. "Human development revisited: A new UNDP report." *World Development* 19 (10): 1469–1473. doi:10.1016/0305-750X(91)90089-Z.

Horsthemke, K. 2015. *Animals and African Ethics*. New York, NY: Palgrave Macmillan. doi:10.1057/9781137504050.

Horsthemke, K. 2017. "Biocentrism, Ecocentrism, and African Modal Relationalism: Etieyibo, Metz, and Galgut on Animals and African Ethics." *Journal of Animal Ethics* 7 (2): 183–188. doi:10.5406/janimalethics.7.2.0183.

Horsthemke, K. 2018. "African Communalism, Persons, and Animals." *Filosofia Theoretica* 7: 60–79.

Hughes, G. 2011. "The Concept of Dignity in the Universal Declaration of Human Rights." *Journal of Religious Ethics* 39 (1): 1–24. doi:10.1111/j.1467-9795.2010.00463.x.

Hurley, P. 1995. "Getting Our Options Clear: A Closer Look at Agent-Centered Options." *Philosophical Studies* 78 (2): 163–188. doi:10.1007/BF00989680.

Ikuenobe, P. 2006. *Philosophical Perspectives on Communalism and Morality in African Traditions*. Lanham, MD: Lexington Books.

Ikuenobe, P. 2015. "Relational Autonomy, Personhood, and African Traditions." *Philosophy East & West* 65 (4): 1005–1029. doi:10.1353/pew.2015.0101.

Ikuenobe, P. 2016. "Good and Beautiful: A Moral-Aesthetic View of Personhood in African Communal Traditions." *Essays in Philosophy* 17 (1): 124–163. doi:10.7710/1526-0569.1546.

Ikuenobe, P. 2017. "The Communal Basis for Moral Dignity: An African Perspective." *Philosophical Papers* 45 (3): 437–469. doi:10.1080/05568641.2016.1245833.

Ikuenobe, P. 2018. "Human Rights, Personhood, Dignity, and African Communalism." *Journal of Human Rights* 17 (5): 589–604. doi:10.1080/14754835.2018.153345 55.

Ilesanmi, O. 2001. "Human Rights Discourse in Modern Africa: A Comparative Religious Perspective." *Journal of Religious Ethics* 23: 293–320.

Imafidon, E. 2013. "On the Ontological Foundation of a Social Ethics in African Traditions." In *Ontologized Ethics: New Essays in African Meta-Ethics*, edited by E. Imafidon and J. Bewaji, 37–54. New York: Lexington Books.

Imafidon, E. 2019. "Intrinsic Versus Earned Worth in African Conception of Personhood." In *Handbook of African Philosophy of Difference. Handbooks in Philosophy*, edited by E. Imafidon, 1–16. Cham: Springer, doi:10.1007/978-3-030-04941-6_11-1.

Iroegbu, P. 2005. "Do All Persons Have a Right to Life?" In *Ethics: General, Special and Professional*, edited by P. Iroegbu and A. Echekwube, 78–83. Ibadan: Heinemann Educational Books.

Jaworska, A., and J. Tannenbaum. 2018. "The Grounds of Moral Status." *The Stanford Encyclopedia of Philosophy*, edited by E. N. Zalta. Accessed 13 October 2019. https://plato.stanford.edu/entries/grounds-moral-status/.

Jones, W. 2001. "Belonging to the ultra-faithful: A response to Eze." *Philosophical Papers* 30 (3): 215–222. doi:10.1080/05568640109485085.

Kant, E. 1996 [1785]. *Groundwork of the Metaphysics of Morals*. Translated by Mary Gregor. Cambridge: Cambridge University Press.

Kaphagawani, D. 2004. "African Conceptions of a Person: A Critical Survey." In *Companion to African Philosophy*, edited by K. Wiredu, 332–442. Oxford: Blackwell Publishing.

Keita, L. 2004. "Philosophy and Development: On the Problematic African Development - A Diachronic Analysis." *Africa Development. Afrique et Developpement* 29: 131–61.

Keurlatz, J. 2012. "The Emergence of Enlightened Anthropocentrism in Ecological Restoration." *Nature and Culture* 7 (1): 48–71. doi:10.3167/nc.2012.070104.

Klaasen, J. 2017. "The Role of Personhood in Development." *Missionalia* 45: 29–44.

Korsgaard, C. 1983. "Two Distinctions in Goodness." *Philosophical Review* 92 (2): 169–195. doi:10.2307/2184924.

Kudadjie, K. 1992. "Towards Moral Development in Contemporary Africa: Insights from Dangme Traditional Moral Experience." In *Person and Community: Ghanaian Philosophical Studies, 1*, edited by K. Wiredu and K. Gyekye, 207–222. Washington, DC: The Council for Research in Values and Philosophy.

Kymlicka, W. 1990. *Contemporary Political Philosophy: An Introduction*. Oxford: Oxford University Press.

LenkaBula, Puleng. 2008. "Beyond Anthropocentricity – Botho/Ubuntu and the Quest for Economic and Ecological Justice in Africa." *Religion and Theology* 15 (3-4): 375–394. doi:10.1163/157430108X376591.

Loewe M. 2012. "Post 2015: How to Reconcile the Millennium Development Goals (MDGs) and the Sustainable Development Goals (SDGs)?" *German Development Institute*. https://post2015.files.wordpress.com/2013/01/loewe-2012-post-2015-mdgs-and-sdgs-english.pdf

Loschke, J. 2017. "Relationships as Indirect Intensifiers: Solving the Puzzle of Partiality." *European Journal of Philosophy* 26 (1): 390–410. doi:10.1111/ejop.12250.

Louw, D. (n.d.). "Power Sharing and the Challenge of Ubuntu Ethics." Pretoria: Research Institute for Theology and Religion. Accessed at http://uir.unisa.ac.za/bitstream/handle/10500/4316/Louw.pdf

Louw, D. 2004. *Ubuntu and the Challenges of Multiculturalism in post-Apartheid South Africa*. Utrecht: Centre for Southern Africa.

Lutz, D. 2009. "African Ubuntu Philosophy and Global Management." *Journal of Business Ethics* 84 (S3): 313–328. doi:10.1007/s10551-009-0204-z.

Mackie, J. 1977. *Ethics: Inventing Right and Wrong*. New York: Penguin.

Macklin, Ruth. 20 Dec, 2003. "Dignity is a useless concept." *BMJ (Clinical Research Ed.)* 327 (7429): 1419–1420. doi:10.1136/bmj.327.7429.1419. PMID:14684633.

Majid, R. 1997. "Towards Post-Development." In *The Post-Development Reader*, edited by R. Majid and V. Bawtree, 377–403. London: Zed Books.

Makwinja, M. 2019. "Human Dignity in Afro-Communitarianism." Doctoral dissertation, University of KwaZulu-Natal, Pietermaritzburg.

Manzini, N. 2018. "Menkiti's Normative Communitarian Conception of Personhood as Gendered, Ableist and Anti-Queer." *South African Journal of Philosophy* 37 (1): 18–33. doi:10.1080/02580136.2017.1405510.

Masaka, D. 2018. "Person, Personhood and Individual Rights in Menkiti's African Communitarian Thinking." *Theoria* 65 (157): 1–14. doi:10.3167/th.2018.6515702.

Masolo, D. 2004. "Western and African Communitarianism: A Comparison." In *Companion to African Philosophy*, edited by K. Wiredu, 483–498 Oxford: Blackwell Publishing.

Masolo, D. 2010. *Self and Community in a Changing World*. Indianapolis: Indiana University Press.

Matolino, B. 2009. "Radicals versus Moderates: A Critique of Gyekye's Moderate Communitarianism." *South African Journal of Philosophy* 28 (2): 160–170. doi:10.4314/sajpem.v28i2.46674.

Matolino, B. 2014. *Personhood in African Philosophy*. Pietermaritzburg: Cluster Publications.

Matolino, B. 2018a. "Restating Rights in African Communitarianism." *Theoria* 65 (157): 57–77. doi:10.3167/th.2018.6515705.

Matolino, B. 2018b. *Consensus as Democracy in Africa*. Grahamstown: NISC. doi:10.2307/j.ctvh8r43s.

Matolino, B., and W. Kwindingwi. 2013. "The End of Ubuntu." *South African Journal of Philosophy* 32 (2): 197–205. doi:10.1080/02580136.2013.817637.

Matolino, B. 2014. *Personhood in African Philosophy*. Pietermaritzburg: Cluster Publications.

Matthews, S. 2004. "Post-development Theory and the Question of Alternatives: A View from Africa." *Third World Quarterly* 25 (2): 373–84. doi:10.1080/0143659 9042000174860.

May, T. 2014. "Moral Individualism, Moral Relationalism and Obligations to Non-human Animals." *Journal of Applied Ethics* 31 (2): 155–168. doi:10.1111/japp.12055.

Mbigi, L. 2005. *The Spirit of African Leadership*. Randburg: Knowers.

Mbiti, J. 1969. *African Religions and Philosophy*. New York, NY: Doubleday.

McNaughton, D., and P. Rawling. 2006. "Deontology." In *Oxford Handbook of Ethical Theory*, edited by D. Copp, 425–458. Oxford: Oxford Press.

McNaughton, D., and P. Rawling. 1992. "Honoring and promoting values." *Ethics* 102 (4): 835–843. doi:10.1086/293451.

Menkiti, I. 1984. "Person and Community in African Traditional Thought." In *African Philosophy: An Introduction*, edited by R. Wright, 171–181. Lanham: University Press of America.

Menkiti, I. 2004. "On the Normative Conception of a Person." In *Companion to African Philosophy*, edited by K. Wiredu, 324–331. Oxford: Blackwell Publishing.

Menkiti, I. 2018. "Person and Community – A Retrospective Statement." *Filosofia Theoretica* 7: 162–167.

Metz, T. 2007. "Toward an African Moral Theory." *Journal of Political Philosophy* 15 (3): 321–41. doi:10.1111/j.1467-9760.2007.00280.x.

Metz, T. 2010. "Human Dignity, Capital Punishment and an African Moral Theory: Toward a New Philosophy of Human Rights." *Journal of Human Rights* 9 (1): 81–99. doi:10.1080/14754830903530300.

Metz, T. 2011. "Ubuntu as a moral theory and human rights in South Africa." *African Human Rights Law Journal* 11: 532–59.

Metz, T. 2012a. "Ethics in Aristotle and in Africa: Some Points of Contrast." *Phronimon* 13: 99–117.

Metz, T. 2012b. "An African Theory of Moral Status: A Relational Alternative to Individualism and Holism." *Ethical Theory and Moral Practice: An International Forum* 14: 387–402. doi:10.1007/s10677-011-9302-y.

Metz, T. 2012c. "African Conceptions of Human Dignity: Vitality and Community as the Ground of Human Rights." *Human Rights Review (Piscataway, N.J.)* 1 (13): 19–37. doi:10.1007/s12142-011-0200-4.

Metz, T. 2013a. "Introduction: Engaging with the Philosophy of D.A. Masolo." *Quest" An African Journal of Philosophy* 25: 7–16.

Metz, T. 2013b. "Two Conceptions of African Ethics." *Quest: An African Journal of Philosophy* 25: 141–162.

Metz, T. 2016. "An Ubuntu-Based Evaluation of the South African State's Responses to Marikana: Where's the Reconciliation?" *Politikon: South African Journal of Political Studies* 44 (2): 287–303. doi:10.1080/02589346.2016.1147192.

Metz, T. 2017. "Replacing Development: An Afro-Communal Approach to Global Justice." *Philosophical Papers* 46 (1): 111–137. doi:10.1080/05568641.2017.1295627.

Michael, Lucy. 2014. "Defining dignity and its place in human rights." *New Bioethics : a Multidisciplinary Journal of Biotechnology and the Body* 20 (1): 12–34. doi:10.1179/2050287714Z.00000000041. PMID:24979874.

Miller, S. 2017. "Reconsidering Dignity Relationally." *Ethics & Social Welfare* 11 (2): 108–121. doi:10.1080/17496535.2017.1318411.

Misztal, B. 2012. "The Idea of Dignity: Its Modern Significance." *European Journal of Social Theory* 16 (1): 101–121. doi:10.1177/1368431012449237.

Mkhandawire, T., and C. Soludo. 1999. "*Our Continent, Our Future: African Perspectives on Structural Adjustment.*" Dakar, Senegal: CODESRIA (Council for the Development of Social Science Research).

Mokgoro, Y. 1998. "Ubuntu and the Law in South Africa." *Potchefstroom Electronic Law Journal* 1: 1–11.

Molefe, M., and C. Allsobrook. 2018. "Editorial: African Philosophy and Rights." *Theoria* 65 (157): v–vii. doi:10.3167/th.2018.6515701.

Molefe, M., and N. Magam. 2019. "What Can Ubuntu Do? A Reflection on African Moral Theory in Light of Post-Colonial Challenges." *Politikon* 46 (3): 311-25. doi:10.1080/02589346.2019.1642669.

Molefe, M. 2011. "What can the Socio-Political Ethic of Ubuntu Contribute to Contemporary Conceptions of Development'?" Masters dissertation, University of the Witwatersrand, Johannesburg.

Molefe, M. 2015a. "Explorations in African Meta-Ethics: Can a Case Be Made for a Supernaturalist Position?" Doctoral dissertation, University of Johannesburg, Johannesburg.

Molefe, M. 2015b. "A Rejection of Humanism in the African Moral Tradition." *Theoria* 63 (143): 59–77. doi:10.3167/th.2015.6214304.

Molefe, M. 2016. "Revisiting the Gyekye-Menkiti Debate: Who is a Radical Communitarian?" *Theoria* 63 (149): 37–54. doi:10.3167/th.2016.6314903.

Molefe, M. 2017a. "A Critique of Thad Metz's African Theory of Moral Status." *South African Journal of Philosophy* 36 (2): 195–205. doi:10.1080/02580136.2016.1203140.

Molefe, M. 2017b. "Individualism in African Moral Cultures." *Cultura: International Journal of Philosophy of Culture and Axiology* 14 (2): 49–68. doi:10.3726/CUL.2017.02.03.

Molefe, M. 2018. "Personhood and (Rectification) Justice In African Thought." *Politikon* 45 (3): 352–367. doi:10.1080/02589346.2018.1435020.

Molefe, M. 2019a. *An African Philosophy of Personhood, Morality and Politics*. New York, NY: Palgrave Macmillan. doi:10.1007/978-3-030-15561-2.

Molefe, M. 2019b (forthcoming). "Solving the Conundrum of African Philosophy Through Personhood: The Individual or Community?" *Journal of Value Inquiry*. doi:10.1007/s10790-019-09683-8.

Molefe, M. 2019c. "Ubuntu and Development: An African Conception of Development." *Africa Today* 66 (1): 96–115. doi:10.2979/africatoday.66.1.05.

Molefe, M. 2019d. "An Environmental Critique of Secular Humanism in African Philosophy." In *African Environmental Ethics*, edited by M. Chemhuru, 55–77. Dordrecht: Springer.

Motlhabi, M., and M. Munyaka. 2009. "Ubuntu and Its Socio-Moral Significance." In *African Ethics: An Anthology of Comparative and Applied Ethics*, edited by F. M. Murove, 324–331. Pietermaritzburg: University of KwaZulu-Natal Press.

Murove, F. 2009. *African Ethics: An Anthology of Comparative and Applied Ethics*. Pietermaritzburg: University of KwaZulu-Natal Press.

Neale, P., and D. Paris. 1990. "Liberalism and the Communitarian Critique: A Guide for the Perplexed." *Canadian Journal of Political Science* 23 (3): 419–439. doi:10.1017/S0008423900012695.

Nel, P. 2008. "Morality and Religion in African Thought." *Acta Theologica (Bloemfontein)* 2: 33≠44.

Norton, B. 1984. "Environmental Ethics and Weak Anthropocentrism." *Environmental Ethics* 6 (2): 131–148. doi:10.5840/enviroethics19846233.

Nussbaum, M. 2011. *Creating Capabilities: The Human Development Approach*. Cambridge, MA: The Belknap Press of Harvard University Press. doi:10.4159/harvard.9780674061200.

O'Neill, O. 1997. "Environmental Values, Anthropocentrism and Speciesism." *Environmental Values* 6 (2): 127–142. doi:10.3197/096327197776679121.

Oelofsen, R. 2018. "Women and Ubuntu: Does Ubuntu Condone the Subordination of Women?" In *African Philosophy and the Epistemic Marginalisation of Women*, edited by J. Chimakonam and L. Du Toit, 42–57. New York: Routledge. doi:10.4324/9781351120104-4.

Okeja, U. 2013. *Normative Justification of a Global Ethic: A Perspective from African Philosophy*. New York, NY: Lexington Books.

Oyowe, A. 2013. "Personhood and Social Power in African Thought." *Alternation (Durban)* 20: 203–228.

Oyowe, A. 2014a. "Fiction, Culture and the Concept of a Person." *Research in African Literatures* 45 (2): 46–62. doi:10.2979/reseafrilite.45.2.46.

Oyowe, A. 2014b. "An African Conception of Human Rights? Comments on the Challenges of Relativism." *Human Rights Review (Piscataway, N.J.)* 15 (3): 329–347. doi:10.1007/s12142-013-0302-2.

Oyowe, A. 2018. "Personhood and Strong Normative Constraints." *Philosophy East & West* 68 (3): 783–801. doi:10.1353/pew.2018.0073.

Oyowe, A., and O. Yurkivska. 2014. "Can a Communitarian Concept of African Personhood be both Relational and Gender-Neutral?" *South African Journal of Philosophy* 33 (1): 85–99. doi:10.1080/02580136.2014.892682.

Pannenberg, W. 1991. *Systematic Theology*. vol. 2. Grand Rapids: William B. Eerdmans.

Paris, P. 1995. *The Spirituality of African Peoples: The Search for a Common Moral Discourse*. Minneapolis: Fortress Press.

Pinker, S. 2008. "The Stupidity of Dignity." *The New Republic*, May 28. https://newrepublic.com/article/64674/the-stupidity-dignity

Pojman, L. 1995. "Theories of Equality: A Critical Analysis." *Behavior and Philosophy* 23: 1–27.

Pojman, L. 2002. "What is Ethics?" In *Ethical Theory: Classic and Contemporary Readings*, edited by L. Pojman, 1–7. London: Wadsworth.

Praeg, L. 2014. *A Report on Ubuntu*. Pietermaritzburg: University of KwaZulu-Natal Press.

Presbey, G. 2002. "Maasai concepts of personhood: The roles of recognition, community, and individuality." *International Studies in Philosophy* 34 (2): 57–82. doi:10.5840/intstudphil200234244.

Rachels, J., and S. Rachels. 2015. *The Elements of Moral Philosophy*. Boston, MA: McGraw Hill.

Ramose, M. 1999. *African Philosophy through Ubuntu*. Harare: Mond Books.

Ramose, M. 2003. "The Ethics of Ubuntu." In *The African Philosophy Reader*, edited by P. Coetzee and A. Roux, 324–331. New York, NY: Routledge.

Ramose, M. 2009. "Towards Emancipative Politics in Africa." In *African Ethics: An Anthology of Comparative and Applied Ethics*, edited by F. Murove. Pietermaritzburg: University of KwaZulu-Natal Press.

Ramose, M. 2010. "The Death of Democracy and the Resurrection of Timocracy." *Journal of Moral Education* 39 (3): 291–303. doi:10.1080/03057240.2010.497610.

Rawls, J. 1971. *A Theory of Justice*. Cambridge: Harvard University Press.

Regan, T. 1987. "The Case for Animal Rights." In *Advances in Animal Welfare Science 1986/87*. vol. 3., edited by M. W. Fox and L. D. Mickley, 179–189. Dordrecht: Springer. doi:10.1007/978-94-009-3331-6_15.

Rodriguez, P. 2015. "Human dignity as an essentially contested concept." *Cambridge Review of International Affairs* 28 (4): 743–756. doi:10.1080/09557571.2015.1021297.

Rosen, M. 2012. *Dignity: Its History and Meaning*. Cambridge, MA: Harvard University Press. doi:10.4159/harvard.9780674065512.

Ryberg, J., T. Peterson, and C. Wolf. 2007. *New Waves in Applied Ethics*. New York: Palgrave Macmillan.

Sebidi, J. 1988. *Towards the Definition of Ubuntu as African Humanism*. Paper. Private Collection.

Segage, M. 2018. "African's development trajectory in a globalised world – Africanism or globalist modernity." *African Journal of Public Affairs* 10: 35–48.

Sen, A. 1987. *On Ethics and Economics*. Oxford: Basil Blackwell Ltd.

Sen, A. 2001. *Development as Freedom*. 2nd ed. Oxford, New York: Oxford University Press.

Shutte, Augustine. 2001. *Ubuntu: An Ethic for a New South Africa*. Pietermaritzburg: Cluster Publications.

Shutte, Augustine. 2009. "Ubuntu as the African Ethical Vision." In *African Ethics: An Anthology for Comparative and Applied Ethics*, edited by Munyaradzi Felix Murove, 85–99. University of KwaZulu-Natal Press.

Singer, P. 2009. "Speciesism and Moral Status." *Metaphilosophy* 40 (3-4): 567–581. doi:10.1111/j.1467-9973.2009.01608.x.

Slote, M. 2010. "A Sentimentalist Moral Education." *Theory and Research in Education* 8 (2): 125–143. doi:10.1177/1477878510368611.

Sober, E. 2001. *Core Questions in Philosophy: A Text with Readings*. New Jersey: Prentice Hall.

Tasioulas, J. 2012. "Towards a Philosophy of Human Rights." *Current Legal Problems* 65 (1): 1–30. doi:10.1093/clp/cus013.

Tempels, P. 1959. *Bantu Philosophy*, Trans. C. King. Paris: Presence Africaine.

Toscano, M. 2011. "Human Dignity as High Moral Status." *The Ethics Forum* 6: 4–25.

Tshivhase, M. 2013. "Personhood: Social Approval or a Unique Identity?" *Quest: An African Journal of Philosophy* 25: 119–140.

Tutu, D. 1999. *No Future without Forgiveness*. New York: Random House. doi:10.1111/j.1540-5842.1999.tb00012.x.

Vale, P., and S. Maseko. 1998. "South Africa and the African Renaissance." *International Affairs* 74 (2): 271–287. doi:10.1111/1468-2346.00016.

Van Niekerk, J. 2007. "In defence of an Autocentric account of Ubuntu." *South African Journal of Philosophy* 26 (4): 364-68. doi:10.4314/sajpem.v26i4.31494.

Van Niekerk, J. 2013. *Ubuntu and Moral Theory*. Johannesburg: University of the Witwatersrand.

Waldron, J. 2012 [2007]. "Dignity and Rank." *Archives Europeennes de Sociologie* 48 (2): 201-37. doi:10.1017/S0003975607000343.

Walker, C. 2013. "Uneasy Relations: Women, Gender, Equality and Tradition." *Thesis Eleven* 115: 77–94. doi:10.1177/0725513612470535.

Wall, S. 2012. "Perfectionism in Moral and Political Philosophy." In *The Stanford Encyclopedia of Philosophy*, edited by E. N. Zalta. Accessed 13 October 2019. https://plato.stanford.edu/entries/perfectionism-moral/.

Warren, A. 1997. *Moral Status: Obligations to Persons and Other Living Things*. Oxford: Clarendon Press.

Wingo, A. 2006. "Akan Philosophy of the Person." In *The Stanford Encyclopedia of Philosophy*, edited by E. N. Zalta. Accessed 13 October 2019. https://plato.stanford.edu/archives/sum2017/entries/akan-person/.

Wiredu, K. 1980. *Philosophy and an African Culture*. Cambridge: Cambridge University Press.

Wiredu, K. 1992. "Moral Foundations of an African Culture." In *Person and Community: Ghanaian Philosophical Studies, 1*, edited by K. Wiredu and K. Gyekye. Washington, DC: The Council for Research in Values and Philosophy.

Wiredu, K. 1996a. *Cultural Universals and Particulars: An African Perspective*. Indianapolis: Indiana University Press.

Wiredu, K. 1996b. "Reply to English/Hamme." *Journal of Social Philosophy* 27 (2): 234–243. doi:10.1111/j.1467-9833.1996.tb00248.x.

Wiredu, K. 2004. "Introduction: African Philosophy in our Time." In *Companion to African Philosophy*, edited by K. Wiredu, 1–27. Oxford: Blackwell Publishing.

Wiredu, K. 2008. "Social Philosophy in Postcolonial Africa: Some Preliminaries Concerning Communalism and Communitarianism." *South African Journal of Philosophy* 27 (4): 332–339. doi:10.4314/sajpem.v27i4.31522.

Wiredu, K. 2009. "An Oral Philosophy of Personhood: Comments on Philosophy and Orality." *Research in African Literatures* 40 (1): 8–18. doi:10.2979/RAL.2009.40.1.8.

Wolf, S. 1992 [1982]. "Moral Saints." *Journal of Philosophy* 79 (8): 419–39. doi:10.2307/2026228.

Wolf, S. 1999. "Morality and the View from Here." *Journal of Ethics* 3 (3): 203–223. doi:10.1023/A:1009833100856.

Wood, A. 2007. "Cross-Cultural Moral Philosophy: Reflections on Thaddeus Metz: 'Toward an African Moral Theory'." *South African Journal of Philosophy* 26 (4): 336–348. doi:10.4314/sajpem.v26i4.31491.

Ziai, A. 2007. "Development Discourse and Its Critics." In *Exploring Post-development*, edited by A. Ziai, 3–17. New York: Routledge. doi:10.4324/9780203962091.

Index

A

'abstract egalitarian plateau' 40
action-centred moral theories 23–24, 33, 33n3
adjustment programmes, Washington consensus 93
African axiological resources 93
African cultures
    animal rights in 86–87
    development in 92–93
    equality of women in 55
African languages
    dignity in 37–39
    sympathy in 50–51, 73n3
African National Congress 105
African philosophy
    animals in 13, 79–85
    dignity in 12, 43–49
    personhood and 2–7
    women in 13, 55
African philosophy and Rights 1
Afro-communitarianism 48, 55
agency 19, 20, 26, 104
agent-centred moral theories 23–24, 33n3
agent-centred notion of personhood 3–7, 10, 17, 33n3, 44, 47–49, 70, 72, 98–99, 115
agent-centred restrictions (constraints) 31–32, 37, 72, 102
agent-centred theory of value 18–27, 115
age (seniority) 60–61
agriculture 75, 90
Ajei, Martin 112n2
Akan people 48, 80
aliens, hypothetical case of 82, 89
Allsobrook, Christopher 1
ancestors 13, 86
animal agriculture 75, 90
animals 75–91, 114–116
    anthropocentrism 76–84, 86–90
    Gyekye, Kwame 84–85
    Menkiti, Ifeanyi 83–84
    Metz, Thaddeus 80–83, 88–89
    moral status of 9, 13–14, 45–47, 107–108, 114–116
    personhood's application to 86–90
    rights of 68–69, 75–76, 83–84, 86–87, 90
    speciesism 76, 78–79, 82–83, 88, 89
    Wiredu, Kwasi 79–80
Animals and African Ethics 86
Annas, Julia 33n3
anthropocentrism 76–84, 86–90, 114
    enlightened 77, 79, 108
    strong 77, 79, 82–84, 89
    weak 77, 79, 81, 87–90, 91n1, 107, 116
apartheid 28, 100, 104–107
'a person is a person through other persons' 10, 18, 21, 22, 65, 98
applied ethics 1–2, 6, 7–9
appraisal respect 4–5, 45, 67
authenticity 29
autonomy 29–30, 47, 64, 70

B

Beauchamp, Tom 7–8
Behrens, Kevin 3–5, 6, 13, 22
being human vs being a person 6, 18–19, 33n2
Biko, Stephen Bantu 94
biocentrism 91n1
black labour, cheap 105–106
Brennan, A. 40

C

capabilities approach 95
capitalism 106
care ethics 51
Catholic view of original sin 19
character-based morality 21–22, 23–24
cheap black labour 105–106
Chemhuru, M. 13

133

Index

children (infants)   16n4, 42–43, 51, 84–85, 86
class   60–61
climate change   108
cohesion   32
'collectivity'   72
colonialism   59, 65, 86, 100, 104–107
common goods   72, 102–107
Communal Basis for Moral Dignity, The   39
communitarianism   5–6, 8, 70, 72
community   8, 26–27, 29–30, 43–44, 57–58, 62–64, 81, 109–111
concept vs conception of moral status   4
consensus   110–111
constraints (agent-centred restrictions)   31–32, 37, 72, 102
cows   101
crocodile, with two heads and one stomach   103
cultural community   57, 62–64
cultural issues   9, 58–60, 62, 64, 96
cultural values   64, 111

D

Darwall, Stephen   4–5
decolonisation   9
DeGrazia, D.   3
dehumanisation   28, 56, 101, 104
Descartes, René   59, 64
development   92–113, 116
    as contested concept   14, 92
    development ethics   94–97
    economism   93–94
    environmental sphere   107–108, 111
    ethics of means   96, 109–111
    good human life   95–96, 97–99
    just societies   95–96, 99–107
    rejection of   92–93
dignified existence   104
dignitas   36, 40
dignity   35–53, 115
    in African languages   37–39
    in African philosophy   43–49
    applied ethics and   8–9
    as contested concept   10–13
    development and   98–99, 100–102, 104–106, 108, 113n6
    equality of women and   56, 70–73
    Gyekye, Kwame   47–49, 51
    Ikuenobe, Polycarp   39–43, 51–52
    Menkiti, Ifeanyi   43–47, 51
    moral status and   36–37
    personhood and   1, 31–32, 35, 115
    place of animals and   81–82
    sympathy and   49–52
Donnelly, Jack   11
Dower, N.   109
duties
    indirect   108, 111
    negative   32, 102, 113n6
    other-regarding   21–22, 29–30, 50, 51, 66–67, 72
    positive   32, 102, 113n6
    strong   37, 113n6

E

economic classes   60–61
economism   93–94, 109, 112n2
'economy of affection'   72
egalitarianism   37, 40–41, 55, 58–62, 67–68, 70–72, 101–102, 114
egoism   25–26, 29
emotions   116
empathy   73n3
engineering approach to development   109
enlightened anthropocentrism   77, 79, 108
entertainment, use of animals for   75, 90
'environing community'   43–44, 58
environmental sphere   77, 95–96, 107–108, 111, 116
equality   12, 37, 40–41
    see also women, equality of
'equal wrongness thesis'   37
ethical naturalism   7, 15, 79–80
ethics   65–66
    see also applied ethics
ethics of means   96, 109–111
Etieyibo, E.   13
'expanding circle' narrative   37
Eze, Michael   62

F

feminism   64, 71, 107
feta kgomo o tsware motho   100–101
Fine, Ben   95
foetuses   13, 16n4
friendship   81

G

gender equality *see* women, equality of
Gilligan, Carol   71
good human life   95–96, 97–99
Goulet, D.   96, 109
Gyekye, Kwame
    common goods   72, 103
    development   103
    dignity   13, 35, 44, 47–49, 51
    equality of women   62–63, 65–66, 70, 72
    morality   20, 21, 22, 23, 27
    personhood   5–6, 10
    place of animals   13–14, 84–85
    social relationships   19

H

harmony   32
hearing   87–88
hedonistic utilitarianism   7
homosexuals   13, 86
Horsthemke, Kai   13, 71, 73n3, 86–87, 89–90
Hughes, Glenn   40–41
'human goods'   103
humanistic approach to ethics   80
humanity formulation (Kant)   28
humanity, recognition of others'   100
humanity, quality of   28
human nature   18–20
human personality   19
human rights   1, 15n1, 41, 68
hunting, of animals   75, 90

I

'I am because we are'   19, 30, 59, 62–63
identity   80–81
Ikuenobe, Polycarp   10, 12–13, 35, 39–43, 51–52
Imafidon, Elvis   13, 73n1
imperialism   59, 96
indirect duties towards environment   108, 111
individualism   24–25, 29–30, 114, 115
individual uniqueness *see* uniqueness
infants (young children)   16n4, 42–43, 51, 84–85, 86
isiXhosa   38
isiZulu   38, 50–51, 73n3

J

justice   44–45
just societies   95–96, 99–107, 108

K

Kant, Immanuel   28, 101
Kaphagawani, Didier   59
Keita, Lansana   99
killing of humans   31–32
Klaasen, John   112n4
Kudadjie, K.   94

L

labour, cheap black   105–106
'last man' objection   82
liberal view of personhood   62–63
literature review   9–14
lived experience of women *see* problems facing women
Louw, Dirk   30
love   81
Lo, Y.   40
Lutz, David   30

M

majoritarianism   110–111
Manzini, Nompumelelo   13, 73n1
Marikana massacre   105–106
Masolo, Dismas   4, 10, 72
maximising of values   31
Mbiti, John   19, 56, 59, 62–64
'means of means'   109
Menkiti, Ifeanyi

Index

agent-centred notion of personhood 4, 21–24
   development 97–98
   dignity 13, 35–36, 43–47, 51
   egoism 25
   equality of women 60, 63, 68–69, 72
   evaluation of philosophy of 114
   'I am because we are' 19
   normative concept of personhood 5–6
   place of animals 13–14, 83–84
   social relationships 26–27, 29
meta-ethics 7, 15, 79–80
Metz, Thaddeus
   concepts of personhood 2–3, 44
   criticism of personhood 31
   development 92, 111
   egoism 25
   equality of women 65
   evaluation of Menkiti's philosophy 114
   human rights 8
   individualism 24
   Marikana massacre 105–106
   place of animals 13, 80–83, 88–89
   right actions 27
   social relationships 16n7
modal-relational view (Metz) 81–82, 88–89
moderate communitarianism 8, 70
modernisation 93
Mokgoro, Yvonne 21, 98
monistic approach 8
moral achievement 4, 39–41
moral egoism 25–26, 29
moral excellence 44, 62, 65, 70
'moral injury' 107
morality 17, 18, 21, 23–25, 28–31, 50, 71, 78–80, 109–110
moral perfection 1, 8–9, 22, 29–33, 66, 72–73, 97–100, 109–110, 115
moral possibilities 28
moral sense, capacity for 46, 84–85
moral-political philosophy (Rawls) 44–45
moral status
   animals and 76–78, 81–82, 84–90
   biocentrism 91n1

   development and 107–108
   dignity and 36–37, 43–49
   equality of women and 67–70
   in personhood 1, 3–4, 8–9
moral theory, personhood as 17–34, 65
moral virtues 3, 48–49, 66–67, 69–70, 85, 87–89
Mothlabi, M. 98, 110
Munyaka, M. 98, 110

N

negative duties 32, 102, 113n6
Nguni language 23–24, 38
Nkrumah, Kwame 14
normative ethics 7
normative notions of personhood 2–5, 18, 56–58, 61–67
Nyerere, Julius 14

O

objects of sympathy, animals as 88, 90, 108
Oelofsen, Rianna 73n2
offenders, reform of 28
Onah, Godfrey 109–110
O'Neill, Onora 78
ontological concept of personhood 2, 18–19, 39, 44–47, 56, 62–65
other-regarding virtues 21–22, 29–30, 50, 51, 66–67, 72
'ought implies can' principle 42–43
Oyowe, Anthony 3, 6, 13, 18, 55–62, 64–67, 70–73, 114

P

Pan Africanism 14
patient-centred notion of personhood 3–7, 35, 45, 48–49, 70
patriarchy 55, 56, 65, 101
perfection see moral perfection
'performative dignity' 52
personal identity 2–3, 43–44
personhood
   in African philosophy 2–7
   as agent-centred theory of value 18–27
   criticisms of 29–33, 114

history of   15n3
  as moral theory   17–34
  as principle of right action   27–28
  ubuntu vs   9–10
Peterson, T.   7
pluralistic approach   8
political work of personhood *see* power, struggle for
positive duties   32, 102, 113n6
power, struggle for   58–61, 65
Praeg, Leonhard   106–107
Presbey, Gail   65
price, Kant's distinction between worth and   101
problems facing women   55–56, 60, 61, 64–65, 71–72
processual nature of personhood   21–22, 44, 57–58
psychological egoism   19

R

racism   101
Ramose, Mogobe   10, 18, 98, 100
rape   28
rationality, Descartes   59, 64
Rawls, John   44–45, 68
recognition respect   4, 45, 46, 67–68, 70
reconciliation   106–107, 111
Regan, Tom   75, 76, 90
'relational autonomy'   64
religious *see* spiritual conceptions
Replacing Development   92
respect   4–5, 12, 39, 42–43, 45–46, 53n3, 67–68, 70
right actions   7, 27–28, 33n3
rights
  animal   68–69, 75–76, 83–84, 86–87, 90
  human   1, 15n1, 41, 68
Rosen, M.   37
Ryberg, J.   7

S

satisficing moral logic   31–32
science, use of animals in   75, 90
Sebidi, J.   20
secular approach   12, 15, 38, 79–80

selfishness   32
self-realisation   8, 16n5, 66, 97–98
self-regarding duties   21–22, 29–30, 32–33, 114
Sen, Amartya   95
seniority (age)   60–61
sentience of animals   76, 88–89, 115
seSotho   23–24, 38, 50–51, 73n3, 100–101
shadows   38
Shutte, Augustine   25, 110
Singer, Peter   75–76
slavery   100
social egalitarianism   12, 61–62
socialisation   57, 60, 63
social justice   67–70
social power   58–61, 65
social relationships
  development and   101, 109–111
  equality of women and   13, 57, 58, 59–64, 66–67, 71
  in personhood   10, 26–27, 30, 32–33
  place of animals and   81
  role of   18–22
social standing   60–61
social transformation   55, 94–95
solidarity   80–81
Sotho language   23–24, 38, 50–51, 73n3, 100–101
South Africa
  apartheid   28, 100, 104–107
  Marikana massacre   105–106
  reconciliation   106–107
'species-apartheid'   86–87, 88
speciesism   76, 78–79, 82–83, 88, 89, 114
spiritual conceptions   12, 15, 25, 38, 47, 70, 79–80, 112n2
'status dignity'   52
stringent constraints   37, 113n6
strong anthropocentrism   77, 79, 82–84, 89
strongly normative idea of personhood   3, 6, 114
structural adjustment programs   93
suffering   76, 78
suffrage, universal   41
sympathy   49–52, 71–74, 87–89, 100, 102, 108, 115–116

Index

T

Theoria: A Journal of Social and Political Theory 1
Theory of Justice 68
transformation of society 55, 94–95
Tshivhase, M. 29
Tutu, Desmond 19, 21, 28

U

ubuntu
    personhood and 9–10
        see also 'a person is a person through other persons'
unconditional respect 12, 39, 42–43, 70
uniqueness 29–30, 32–33, 114, 115
United Nations Development Programmes 96
utilitarianism 23

V

values 56–57, 64, 94, 111
virtues 8, 21–22, 47–52, 66–67, 69–71, 98, 115–116
vitality 8, 38, 110

W

Waldron, J. 36
Warren, Anne 3
Washington consensus 93
weak anthropocentrism 77, 79, 81, 87–90, 91n1, 107, 116
weakly normative notion of personhood 3
Western cultures 6, 9, 12, 59, 92–93, 112n3
Wiredu, Kwasi
    development 111
    dignity 31–32

equality of women 60, 66, 70
personhood 4, 5, 9, 10
place of animals 79–80
sympathy 50, 73n3
values 21–22
Wolf, C. 7
Wolf, Susan 31
women, equality of 13, 54–74, 114–115
    just societies 101–102
    moral status 67–70
    normative notions of personhood 61–67
    ontological idea of personhood 62–65
    Oyowe's and Yurkivska's definition of personhood 55–56, 57–58
    Oyowe's argument 58–61, 62, 64–65, 67
    problems facing women 55–56, 60, 61, 64–65, 71–72
    response to Oyowe's criticisms 70–73
    social egalitarianism 61–62
    social justice 67–70
worth, Kant's distinction between price and 101
wrong actions 7, 27–28

X

Xhosa language 38

Y

young children (infants) 16n4, 42–43, 51, 84–85, 86
Yurkivska, Olga 13, 55–58

Z

Zulu language 38, 50–51, 73n3

www.ingramcontent.com/pod-product-compliance
Lightning Source LLC
Chambersburg PA
CBHW060456300426
44113CB00016B/2609